D1514932

Book Theft and Library Security Systems, 1981-82

by Alice Harrison Bahr

Knowledge Industry Publications, Inc.
White Plains, New York 10604

Professional Librarian Series

Book Theft and Library Security Systems, 1981-82

by Alice Harrison Bahr

Library of Congress Cataloging in Publication Data

Bahr, Alice Harrison.
    Book theft and library security systems,
1981-82.

    (Professional librarian)
    Bibliography: p.
    Includes index.
    1.   Libraries—Security measures.   2.   Book
thefts.   I. Title.   II. Series.
Z679.6.B333   025.8 '2.   80-26643
ISBN 0-914236-71-7 (pbk.)

Printed in the United States of America

Table of Contents

List of Tables and Figures

Photographs

I

Introduction:
The Ubiquitous Thief

*Book losses in your library probably aren't as bad as you think.
More than likely, they are much worse.*[1]

In the library world reports of collection losses and annual loss rates began to appear in print with some frequency in the late 1960s. Shortly after the middle of the decade, for example, the Suffolk County Senior High School reported that 22.7% of its newly acquired books had disappeared from the shelves.[2] In 1969 Carnegie Mellon University Library announced a 10.2% collection loss.[3] A 1973 inventory at the C.W. Post Center Library of Long Island University revealed a collection loss of 10%.[4] Then in 1975 the Virginia Western Community College Library (Roanoke, VA) reported an annual loss of approximately 700 books.[5] Often more startling than long-term collection losses, annual losses gave libraries a clearer picture of how much book theft was costing them. Whether reports accounted for long-term or annual losses, they were usually accompanied by discussions about the newest theft-detection device—the electronic security system—and within a few years librarians declared the 1970s the age of electronic security. The description is likely to be even more fitting for the 1980s.

SALES INCREASES AND SYSTEM IMPROVEMENTS

In March of 1980 Richard Boss estimated that there were more than 2500 electronic detection systems at work in American libraries and that 500 were leased or sold annually,[6] sure confirmation of Ida Vincent's 1978 generalization that "electronic security systems are increasingly being employed to combat the problem of book thefts from libraries."[7] If worldwide library installations are included, the figure is higher—6600 as of 1979.[8]

The reasons for increasing sales are obvious. In use for more than 15 years, electronic security systems have been proven effective. The literature also reports their cost effectiveness. Published reports of collection losses as well as successes with electronic systems have encouraged libraries to determine their losses, and those startling figures have spurred sales. The installation of an electronic security system is now almost routine in new library buildings.

A further encouragement to sales is vendor response to system shortcomings. All systems operate similarly and have similar components: targets and control units. The former, sensitized strips or tags affixed to library materials, trigger alarms if not desensitized or shielded before patrons exit between two sensing screens (two columns defining exit patterns and containing detection apparatus). The latter are controls for power supply, alarm type and duration, etc. Librarians have asked for (1) smaller, less detectable targets; (2) special targets for audiovisual (A/V) materials; (3) less obtrusive sensing columns; (4) fewer false alarms; and (5) more affordable prices. Over the last two years most vendors have decreased target size, making targets more workable with A/V materials; several have improved systems; and a few have lowered prices.

Changes in design are ongoing. In 1979 Checkpoint introduced the Mark III, a third-generation system with smaller, more streamlined sensing screens and with other technical improvements. In 1980 the Knogo Mark II was replaced by the Mark IV, with smaller sensing screens and a modified control panel; the Knogo Mark V, with redesigned sensing screens, will be introduced in 1981. Also in 1981 Gaylord plans to demonstrate a second-generation system with much smaller, pillar-shaped sensing screens. In the fall of 1980 Sensormatic began testing a new magnetic security system at a Florida library.

In some cases streamlining has brought prices down, or at least held them at the same level. The Checkpoint Mark III is no more expensive than the Mark II, although it is smaller and designed to eliminate any system compromise previously effected by carrying library material through sensing screens in a particular manner. 3M's new security systems, the 1850, 1350 and 1250, are considerably less expensive than previous Tattle-Tape and Spartan models. The 1850, for example, is about two inches narrower, five inches shorter and costs $1400 less than the Tattle-Tape system. The newest model, the 1350, is even smaller and less expensive than the 1850. One impetus behind Gaylord's redesign is to offer a more economical system.

EXTENT OF LIBRARY LOSSES

While electronic security systems are neither the only nor necessarily the best means of insuring the safety of all collections, the steady increase in their installation reflects a growing awareness of the extent of library losses. On all levels—international, national and local—the statistics are alarming. In 1978 council libraries in the United Kingdom lost an estimated 3% to 10% of their stock. According to the *Municipal Journal*, those losses cost libraries between £15 million and £25 million.[9] In the same year Scottish libraries set the cost of annual losses at £1 million.[10] Without mentioning figures, even Russian libraries admitted to spiraling library stock losses in 1979.[11]

By 1978 Canadian secondary schools set annual losses at between 2% and 15% of their total collections.[12] For American high school libraries the annual loss is somewhere between 5% and 10% of the total collections.[13] The most dismaying study of American college library loss, *Fair Practice in Higher Education,* was released in 1979 by the Carnegie Council on Policy Studies in Higher Education. Its conclusion was that book theft is a serious problem for most college libraries.[14] Even a cautious estimate of nationwide library collection loss indicates the magnitude of the problem. If the average book costs $15 to replace, then replacing 1% of the country's estimated 1.5 billion volumes costs American libraries $225 million—more than 10% of what they spend annually.

While national loss figures are impressive, individual reports most disturb administrators faced with shrinking budgets, rising book costs and growing desiderata files (books the library would like to purchase if funds were available). Losses at individual institutions may be much higher than the national averages. For example, the New York Public Library estimates its annual loss at 10%.[15] The Rochester Public Library (Rochester, NY) loses 15% of total acquisitions each year, approximately $33,750 in 1979.[16] Long-term losses also indicate the high cost of book theft to the individual library. The Tucson (AZ) Public Library's Woods branch recently reported a 17% book stock loss; at the Wellesley (MA) Free Library, the loss was 20% in 15 years.[17,18] An inventory of the Harvey S. Firestone Memorial Library, Princeton University's principal library building, revealed the following losses: 12.5% of the 40,000 titles essential to teaching programs, and more than 4.3% of the almost 2 million volumes in Firestone's open stacks. Princeton calculates replacement expenses for all missing items at $3 million.[19]

Why Theft Is Increasing

Escalating prices for books in general and rare books in particular provide one explanation for such expensive losses. According to *Publishers Weekly,* the overall average price of hardcover volumes increased about 13.4% from 1978 to 1979. The average price of a hardcover volume in 1979, even after volumes priced at $81 or more were eliminated from calculations, was $18.95.[20]

The increased value of rare books and manuscripts attracts the professional thief. In 1973 two "self-styled Byzantine priests" pilfered the collections of Fordham, Yale and Harvard.[21] In the middle of the decade, a number of academic libraries in the northeast reported the disappearance of Winslow Homer prints from 19th-century journals. Cornell University lost 156 prints.[22] In 1978 two Americans pulled a bizarre caper. Setting up Mexico City post office box numbers for bogus institutions, they used normal interlibrary loan channels to amass more than 300 books.[23] (The culprits were arrested one year later.) In 1979 Carleton College (Northfield, MN) announced the theft of 153 rare volumes.[24] In 1980 the Federal Bureau of Investigation was called in to investigate the loss of 150 rare books and 200 illustrations from the library at Harvard University 's Museum of Comparative Zoology.[25]

Theft of Nonbook Items

Books are not the sole target of library theft. Audiovisual software and hardware attract both the professional thief and the ordinary library patron. By using fictitious names to obtain library cards, members of a national hot-films ring made off with 19 films from

Ohio libraries and several more from other U.S. libraries.[26] The availability on video cassettes of feature films like *The French Connection* and *The Robe* (distributed by Magnetic Video for Twentieth Century Fox for between $30 and $90), along with librarians' growing commitment to video and increased sales of home video cassette recorders, earmark video materials as potentially high-loss library items.

Pittsburgh's Carnegie Library lost 11 music scores, some rare and valuable, in 1977; the early estimate of loss was $3000.[27] According to the Carnegie Commission, journal mutilation is a serious problem in most American college libraries.[28]

The Library Department of The City College of New York reported lost typewriters and a missing filmstrip reader, but its most phenomenal loss was a $3700 OCLC terminal.[29] That theft is matched by only one other: the disappearance of a piano from the Noe branch of the San Francisco Public Library in 1979.[30] Another unusual incident, thought to be a student prank, was the December 1978 theft of a massive Christmas wreath decorating one of the famous pair of stone lions at the entrance to the New York Public Library. One year later, the wreath mysteriously reappeared—but a second wreath, from the other lion's neck, vanished in the middle of the night.[31]

PLANNING A SECURITY PROGRAM

So much theft requires remedial action. But it demands much more; a security program that meets the needs of the individual institution and its clientele. The following questions should help library managers to devise such a program—one compatible with long-range library goals, library budget, philosophy of service, and staff and collection size:

1. What is the extent of overall collection loss attributable to theft?

2. What is the annual loss rate attributable to theft?

3. What materials are most susceptible to theft?
   - current imprints
   - books in particular subject fields
   - journals

4. How much is theft costing the library? Take into consideration
   - the percentage of books missing because of theft that the library would actually replace
   - additional interlibrary-loan transactions necessitated because of theft
   - additional reference hours wasted because of theft

5. Are losses significant enough to warrant a theft-prevention program?

6. What funds are available for devising and maintaining a theft-prevention program?

7. Which theft-prevention program is most suited to the library budget, library staff, library building design and the nature and extent of losses sustained?

No single publication can answer the final question. However, the goal of this report is to supply data that will help librarians arrive at their own answers. In reading the descriptions of theft-prevention programs that follow, note the environment in which a program is successful and each system's limitations.

Every theft-prevention program has its shortcomings. Anyone who has watched a tired library guard wave crowds of library patrons through check-out lines without looking for date-due cards or going through briefcases knows how the guard system can be compromised. Electronic security systems range from 70% to 95% effective, and all of them can be compromised in some fashion. (The most common way is to remove from books the sensitized targets that trigger alarms.)

Clearly, then, there is no definitive solution to the problem of theft. There are, however, a number of ways to reduce losses significantly. With few exceptions a dedicated, security-conscious staff insures the success of any theft-prevention program. Confidence of that kind, however, results from having chosen the program that best suits the library's individual needs. To be assured that the confidence is well placed, all programs should be evaluated after a year of operation.

FOOTNOTES

1. J.W. Griffith, "Library Thefts: A Problem That Won't Go Away," *American Libraries,* April 1978, p. 224.

2. William J. Greaney, *An Investigation Into the Problem of Lost and Damaged Books in the Senior High School Libraries of Suffolk County,* Thesis, Brookville, NY: Long Island University, 1967.

3. Florine Fuller and Irene Glaus, "To Have or Not To Have a Security System," *Tennessee Librarian,* Spring 1974, p. 41.

4. Donald L. Ungarelli, "Excerpts—Taken from a Paper Entitled The Empty Shelves," *Bookmark,* May-June 1973, p. 155.

5. "Roanoke and Southwest Virginia: Security Systems and Other Activities," *Virginia Librarian,* October 1975, p. 12.

6. Richard W. Boss, "The Library Security Myth," *Library Journal,* March 15, 1980, p. 683.

7. Ida Vincent, "Electronic Security Systems in Libraries: Measuring the Costs and Benefits," *The Australian Library Journal,* September 1978, p. 231.

8. Nancy H. Knight, "Theft Detection Systems for Libraries Revisited: An Updated Survey," *Library Technology Reports,* May-June 1979, p. 221.

9. "Losses Demand Electronics", *Library Association Record,* July 1978, p. 323.

10. Sergeant Alex Shearer, "Essentials of Library Security—The Police View," *SLA News,* 1978, p. 45.

11. A. Pavlodarskii, "A Law for All," *Bibliotekár* (Moscow), 1979, p. 48.

12. Sharon Mott, "An Edmonton High School Reduces Book Losses," *Canadian Library Journal,* February 1978, p. 45.

13. "Quick! Tell Me How to Buy Library Security Systems," *American School Board Journal,* August 1977, p. 43.

14. "Security in Libraries," *Library Journal,* June 1, 1979, p. 1206.

15. Griffith, *op. cit.,* p. 225.

16. "Rochester Pegs Book Losses," *Library Journal,* March 15, 1980, p. 668.

17. "Security in Libraries," *Library Journal,* April 15, 1979, p. 878.

18. Griffith, *op. cit.,* p. 225.

19. "Princeton Cuts Acquisitions; Theft on the Upswing," *Library Journal,* May 1, 1978, p. 917.

20. Chandler B. Grannis, "1979 Title Output and Average Prices," *Publishers Weekly,* February 22, 1980, pp. 54, 57.

21. "Library Security Roundup," *Library Journal,* May 15, 1973, p. 1533.

22. "Libraries Hit by Book and Art Thefts," *Library Journal,* July 1977, pp. 1446-47.

23. "Busting the Mexico City Connection," *American Libraries,* May 1979, p. 224.

24. "Minnesota's Carleton College Reports Rare Book Theft," *Library Journal,* May 15, 1979, p. 1097.

25. "Loss of Rare Books Probed at Harvard," *Chronicle of Higher Education,* March 24, 1980, p. 7.

26. "Security in Libraries," *Library Journal,* November 15, 1978, p. 2292.

27. "Music Scores Stolen from Pittsburgh's Carnegie," *Library Journal,* July 1977, p. 1447.

28. "Security in Libraries," *Library Journal,* June 1, 1979, p. 1206.

29. "Nail Down Your OCLC Terminals," *Library Journal,* June 1, 1979, p. 1207.

30. "Theft in San Francisco," *Library Journal,* June 1, 1979, p. 1207.

31. Telephone conversation with Gerald Gold, Business Manager, New York Public Library, October 24, 1980.

II

Measuring Book Loss

Librarians can measure book loss in a number of ways. The most frequently employed methods, however, are:

- the book census, or gross inventory
- the inventory
- the sample

Each approach can be useful to all sizes and types of libraries. Yet each has its weaknesses and strengths, and the librarian must determine which method matches the library's specific overall objectives more closely.

THE BOOK CENSUS

In 1917 the St. Louis Public Library, employing a staff of 153, calculated its annual book-loss rate in less than five hours.[1] That was no small task for a library containing nearly 500,000 volumes; a book census made it possible. A book census, sometimes called a gross inventory, is a count of the number of volumes either on the library shelves or otherwise accountable for (in processing, binding, circulation or mending, etc.). If existing statistical records of holdings are accurate or if inventories have established the number of books actually owned by the library, the book census supplies a figure that can be subtracted from the actual number of volumes recorded on official records, to determine book loss.

What are the strong points of the book census? First, it has been proven a reliable and accurate method for determining book loss. After a book census was conducted at the Levittown Public Library, an inventory was taken to test its reliability. The inventory indicated a yearly loss of 3.4%; the book census indicated a yearly loss of 3.6%.[2] Second, a book census takes a relatively small amount of time. Third, it provides an accurate volume count, which may differ from the library's record of holdings.

Although a book census is reliable and takes little time, it must be done while the library is closed, and it will indicate only the *number* of volumes missing, not the specific authors and titles. If neither of these qualifications is a problem, the book census is a viable method for calculating book loss. How frequently should it be done? Five-year intervals are recommended. Some authorities suggest taking one every two years.

Conducting a book census calls for careful planning. All books should be shelved, specific shelf-counting assignments by classification number should be made, and a scheduled closing time for the library must be determined. According to current estimates, 2000 books can be counted in an hour. Therefore, if the estimated collection size is 250,000 volumes, 125 working hours are needed to complete the shelf count. If 10 staff members are available the job will take each of them 12 1/2 hours; with 20 staff members, 6 1/4 hours each. Separate assignments will have to be made to count items in circulation, processing, binding and other locations. Much of this work, however, could be performed late Saturday night if the library is closed then, and the shelf-counting could be done on Sunday, again if the library is closed.

Before assignments are scheduled, some agreement must be reached about what to count. For example, if bound periodicals and unbound periodicals are to be included, the counters should be informed. For purposes of uniformity, slips with designated classification numbers should be distributed to workers prior to counting; for example:

Call Number Area	Number of Volumes

Obviously, for the method to work the library must have an accurate tabulation of volumes owned. Fortunately, the St. Louis Public Library had such a tabulation; it had been taking inventories yearly. Other libraries, not so fortunate, could rely on available statistical records of holdings, but to do so would be risky. Sheridan's study, made in 1969-70 at the Levittown (NY) Public Library, showed a 7% inaccuracy in book stock statistics.[3] This inaccuracy had arisen in a 20-year period.

What, then, is a library to do if no previous inventory has been taken? Two options exist. At Levittown a decision was made to count the shelflist. The number of volumes indicated by each shelflist card was recorded and a final tally was taken. The number of volumes physically present was then subtracted from that tally to determine book losses. The other alternative is to take two censuses. The first would establish the number of items physically present in the library. If new acquisitions were added to that, then one year later the figures from the second count could be subtracted from it. If extra books appeared (books borrowed without authorization during the first count but returned by the second), the figures for the first census would have to be revised.

If a second census or a shelflist count is mandatory, costs accelerate accordingly. For the St. Louis Public Library, which did not face this problem, 153 staff members counted 500,000 volumes in 4 1/4 hours. This indicates that a staff of 31 could count 100,000 volumes in the same amount of time. The costs of the operation equal the hourly salary of each counter multiplied by the number of hours worked. Such a sum could be substantial; however, compensatory time could be given in lieu of overtime and the cost could thus be absorbed.

In Levittown, where no reliable statistics were available, costs were higher because of the necessity for counting the shelflist. The time breakdown for each part of the census was as follows (average time per thousand items):

- counting items in the shelflist — 43 minutes
- counting books on the shelf — 35 minutes
- counting items in circulation — 93 minutes[3]

Again total costs are determined by multiplying the number of work hours by the hourly salary of each worker. In St. Louis, total man-hours were 650 1/4; if the hourly wage plus benefits is $4, the cost would be $2601. Of course, the out-of-pocket expense would only be the cost of those hours that the staff would not have worked anyway.

THE INVENTORY

An inventory is a systematic stock-taking that seeks to locate every volume that a library's records show it owns.

Taking a regular, periodic inventory was common practice for public libraries in the 1930s. Today, however, few public libraries take regular, complete inventories, because, as one public library administrative handbook puts it, "experience has shown that loss rates are low . . . and the cost of a complete inventory of a large or medium-sized library is high."[4] While the practice still exists—for example, the Ontario Ministry of Education mandates annual inventories of school library materials—the majority of libraries have abandoned it.[5] In 1977 Thomas L. Welch, associate director of the California State Polytechnic University Library (Pomona, CA), summed up the position of academic libraries: "Generally, academic libraries have abandoned the previously widespread practice of conducting a regular and systematic inventory of their collections."[6]

In 1969 Pamela Bluh, assistant serials librarian at Johns Hopkins University Library, was unable to find much in the way of descriptions of inventories or guidelines in the library literature.[7] In 1975 Bill Bolte, head librarian at Bowling Green (KY) Public Library, reviewed the literature and concluded, "Library literature indicates apathy on the part of librarians regarding inventory."[8] As late as 1977 Catherine V. Von Schon, English bibliographer at the State University of New York at Stony Brook library commented—in what is almost a classic understatement—"Library literature on inventories is not plentiful."[9] While the American Library Association (ALA) has conducted several surveys of library inventory practices, it has neither issued guidelines nor suggested standards for taking inventories.

The apathy is not confined to the United States. D.N. Banerjee of the Indian Institute of Technology in Kanpur wrote:

> We do not generally find a common guide in inventory control of library reading materials. We seldom find a clear-cut procedure in the literature. The library experts have given much thought to library classification, cataloguing, readers service and similar activities but it seems that no serious attempt has been [made in this respect] so far.[10]

The assumptions that losses are low, that full knowledge of all missing books is unessential and that inventories are costly are not necessarily true. As early as 1927, for example, the ALA's survey of inventory practices in U.S. libraries reported:[11]

- In public libraries with more than 100,000 volumes, 26% to 46% of adult fiction books were missing.

- In public libraries with 50,000-100,000 volumes, 17% to 45% of adult fiction books were missing.

- In public libraries with 20,000-50,000 volumes, 10% to 48% of adult fiction books were missing.

The statistics for adult nonfiction and juvenile fiction were equally devastating; only reference collections were spared. Although these astronomical figures do not specify an annual loss rate (nor do they show whether missing books were stolen or just "borrowed"), they are sufficiently large to disprove the notion that book losses were low at some point in the distant past. Today the statistics speak for themselves: *Library Journal* received so many reports of thefts in 1977 that in an article entitled "Security" in the July 1977 issue, it bemoaned the increasing frequency with which libraries are becoming the targets of thieves. Since then "Security in Libraries" has become a regular news feature of the magazine, and the usual news is that library theft is on the upswing.

ALA's 1927 survey attributed decreasing interest in taking inventory, in part, to the notion that lost books that were not reported missing were not needed. We would argue that a library replacing only those books that patrons indicate are missing serves a very small part of its public. Many people rely on the card catalog, not the staff, and if patrons repeatedly cannot find items on the shelves that are listed in the catalog, they will eventually lose confidence in the library.

Inventory taking is an expensive way of determining book loss, yet only the inventory will supply the authors and titles of all volumes that are missing. The expense of gathering these data can be mitigated somewhat if the inventory is part of the preparation for a project other than security, such as moving into a new building, converting holdings records to machine-readable form for an automated circulation system or improving reader services by correcting card-catalog inaccuracies. Library objectives aside, overall costs must also take into consideration collection size and mode of taking inventory.

Inventory Guidelines

Once the library has decided it should take an inventory, it should carefully list all the decisions to be made in order to do the job thoroughly and efficiently. The following checklist can be a starting point.

1. Determine the inventory's goals. Should it:

- weed the collection,

- identify books requiring mending,

- identify mislabeled books,

- verify accession and/or call numbers,

- produce a list of books requiring special attention, e.g., leather-bound books,

- calculate book loss to determine whether a theft program is needed, to test the efficiency of a present theft program, or to determine replacement budget?

2. Decide what part of the collection is to be inventoried:

- For several reasons serials, newspapers, audiovisual materials and documents are usually inventoried separately. They may, for example, be classified in systems other than that used for monographs, and separately housed. In some cases they may be supervised by particular staff members who would like to control the manner in which they are inventoried.

- The Society of American Archivists recommends that rare books and manuscripts be inventoried regularly. "Good legal practice suggests that institutions should make every effort to verify the presence of particularly valuable items at least once every three years. Such inventories are excellent proof of ownership."[12]

- Reference collections should be inventoried annually. Annual inventories familiarize the staff with the collection, provide ever-needed shelf space by eliminating infrequently used reference titles, etc., and indicate the collection's weak areas.

- Annual inventories are recommended for libraries with collections of 50,000 volumes or less.

3. Construct an inventory design that accomplishes all of the inventory's purposes.

4. Determine whether to close the library during inventory.

5. Determine the time available for the inventory.

6. Determine staff available and additional staff necessary to conduct the inventory in the available time.

7. Calculate costs.

8. Before the inventory is started, the appropriate, clearly defined procedural steps should be described in writing and copies distributed to the entire inventory staff.

How to Conduct an Inventory

Once the library has settled on the objectives and procedures for the inventory, the next step is to organize the staff to check physically for the presence of books and other materials. The following section describes this process.

The Basic Process

Step One: Checking the Shelves

- In these days of accelerating labor costs, libraries are trying to cut inventory costs by having a single staff member check the shelves for materials listed in the shelf-list. Formerly, checking the shelves was usually done by teams of two. Unless automation makes possible a printout of library materials, the shelflist drawer is taken to the appropriate library location. When two people are used, one person, holding the shelflist drawer, reads a call number while the second person locates the book on the shelves.

- The person checking for books may actually be doing several jobs. He may be:

    - checking a book's condition,
    - verifying accession number,
    - checking a label's visibility,
    - placing a check or date by the accession number on the shelflist card and/or in the book.

    The last step is a safety measure. Although it takes extra time to inscribe a check or date mark, the inscription is proof that a book has been inventoried.

- The person reading call numbers must process the information received from the shelf checker (except when a single staff member does both jobs). If a book is on the shelves the reader may place a check or date by the accession number for safety purposes; he may also insert a slip routing the book to mending, circulation (non-library material) or cataloging (e.g., to correct a call-number error, to discard the book, to supply a missing shelflist, to be relabeled). Or the checker may fill out an inventory control card (see Figure II-1) listing corrections to be made, and materials can be routed to departments in the future. (This card can also be used in conjunction with routing slips.)

Figure II-1. Inventory Control Card

Call	Main	No sl	
Number	Entry	Repair	
		Relabel	
Volumes on shelves when there is no		Discard	
shelflist card		Dummy	
Notes		Circulation	
		Mender's, etc.	
		2nd Shelf Check	
		2nd Circ. Check	
		O.K.	

If, however, a book is not on the shelves the reader may:

- turn the shelflist card up (call number up),
- place a capital M by the accession number and turn the card up,
- place a clip on the card and turn the card up.

Step Two: Compiling a List of Missing Volumes

- Missing volumes may be recorded in the following fashion:

  - The turned-up cards in the shelflist may be photocopied.

  - The call numbers, authors, titles, copies and volumes on turned-up shelflist cards may be recorded on separate pieces of paper or on a list (though this is unlikely to be done because of the high cost in staff time).

  - The inventory card, filled out by the reader in step one, eliminates step two.

Step Three: Checking Circulation Records

- After checking for items on library shelves and identifying those not found by either turning up shelflist cards or marking inventory cards, the checker should consult the circulation files. If a volume not on the shelves is in circulation, the checker returns the shelflist card to the shelflist drawer or crosses out the photocopy of the shelflist card. If an inventory card was used, the circulation and o.k. blocks should be checked.

Step Four: Checking Additional Files and Locations

- Some libraries mark special designations such as "bindery" on shelflist cards prior to inventorying. Additionally they may interfile circulation records in the shelflist. In line with these steps, these libraries usually cease cataloging new books two weeks before an inventory; this reduces snags and permits time to mark the shelf-list. If these preliminary steps are not taken, missing volumes will have to be checked for on cataloging trucks, on cataloging shelves, on menders' lists or shelves and in any other special locations.

Step Five: Waiting Period/Second Shelf Check

- R.E. Beck and J.R. McKinnon suggest that a second search for missing books be made after sufficient time has elapsed for circulation staff to reshelve books which had been lying on tables, or had been returned but not carded and reshelved prior to the inventory.[13] For their library of over 500,000 volumes, four to seven days were required; the waiting period, however, depends on collection size, staff size and library-use patterns.

Step five is optional if:

- returns are not substantial;

- the library is closed during inventory, and prior to inventory all books were shelved and all returned books were placed on circulation trucks in call-number order for easy checking against the shelflist;

- circulation is automated. Online circulation systems record transactions immediately. If the system is not online, printouts of circulation records should be checked.

Note: Step five is not designed to locate books which were "temporarily stolen"—returned after not being checked out properly. In some libraries this kind of return is substantial. Rechecking shelves for this material might be done frequently, probably every six months, not a few days after an inventory. Usually this "third" shelf check is made after a list of missing books has been compiled and is being reviewed for replacement.

These are the basic steps. However, much more needs to be considered. Library policies and modes of operation may modify any of the basic steps.

Variations of the Inventory Process

The Sample Inventory

Since materials used frequently are those most subject to theft, one way to gauge loss is to inventory only those sections of the collection that receive the greatest use. This is precisely what librarians at Cornell University did in 1977. Based on the percentage of each classification in circulation at a peak period of the fall semester, nine classes of books—a total of 16,146 volumes—were inventoried.[14] Results were tabulated as follows:

B350-398	Vols. on Shelf	Vols. in Circ.	Vols. Missing	Total Vols.	% Missing
Plato	582	48	25	655	3.82%

The advantages and disadvantages of Cornell's method are obvious. It does, as Cornell had hoped, indicate "losses at their worst."[15] Also, it pinpoints authors and titles—giving full bibliographic data—of many missing high-demand materials. What it does not do is indicate the full extent of library loss. Further, it is more expensive and time-consuming than a sample—few samples require checking 16,000 volumes. However, it makes moot the question of whether or not to close the library for inventory purposes.

Closing the Library

A library need not close to conduct an inventory; nevertheless, certain benefits accrue to those that do:

- No new books circulate; therefore Step Five can be eliminated from the basic inventory processes. The circulation file needs to be checked only once.

- Traffic is minimal; patrons are not removing boks from shelves for browsing or for reference.

- The library staff can devote its time completely to the inventory.

- Books may be routed to labeling, repair or cataloging for quick corrections without disrupting services to library patrons.

- The inventory will take less time.

Because of these benefits the Enoch Pratt Free Library in Baltimore closed for its 1955 inventory, the East Chicago (IN) Public Library closed for its 1962 inventory, and the California State Polytechnic University Library closed for its 1977 inventory.

Universities operating on the quarter semester system would find closing the library difficult. Leaving the library open during inventory simply means that the basic inventory cannot be completed in a few days. It will take months or sometimes years, depending on staff size, collection size and technology.

In the early 1950s the University of Washington Libraries conducted a continuous, on-going inventory with the library open; in the early 1970s the University of Guelph (Ont.) Library did the same. The 600,000 volumes at the University of Washington were inventoried in 21 months by 5 1/2 clerks.[16] However, the University of Guelph's 284,455 volumes were inventoried in three months by eight students.[17] Automation cut inventory costs in half at Guelph.

Photographic Charging

The impossibility of closing library doors is not the only deterrent to taking inventory. Photographic charging (the process of taking a picture both of materials charged out and a borrower's library card) also presents an obstacle. Since circulation records are not developed until a certain number of transactions have been completed, the library may not have circulation records against which to check "suspected" missing books.

The Enoch Pratt Free Library in Baltimore solved the problem of taking inventory when circulation records are not available.[18] Fortunately, it had maintained the practice of typing book cards for its volumes. Originally designed as a back-up safety measure in case the photographic charging system failed, the cards made it possible to build up a circulation file. Libraries that have discontinued use of book cards would have to prepare cards for each circulating item to build up such a file.

Automation

Cunliffe reports that prior to automation, libraries of more than 100,000 volumes were advised not to conduct inventories. A 1958 survey of inventory practices indicated that librarians felt the disadvantages of taking inventory far outweighed the advantages. The experience of the University of Guelph in 1972, previously described, indicates how automation can simplify the process of taking inventory. The total cost in this case was under $10,000 and there was no disruption of service to library users while the inventory was conducted.[19]

Optical scanning sheets took the place of the shelflist. Call number, author, title, copy, volume and location symbols were recorded on the sheets. Shelf readers marked the first column if a book was on the shelves and the second if a book was missing. The scanning sheets eliminated the traditional two-man inventory team. After the lists were marked they were run against circulation files, also automated, and a printout of missing books was produced. The shelves were double-checked and a final printout of missing volumes was produced.

One year after the University of Guelph inventory, the State University of New York at Stony Brook library calculated book loss as a by-product of converting holdings to machine-readable form for the automation of circulation. After cards were keypunched, staff went to the stacks to insert cards in library materials. If items were neither in the stacks nor in circulation, they were assumed lost, at least for the moment. As part of the same process, books for which no cards had been prepared were taken to keypunching. According to library estimates, taking cards to the stacks (in newer systems bar-coded or OCR labels would be taken to the stacks) is four times faster than the usual process of carrying the shelflist into the stacks and having one person read call numbers and another check the shelves. Instead of 10 minutes for 1 inch of cards, only 2½ minutes are necessary.[20]

Automation makes taking inventory of the large collection easier, and it helps to dispel the myth that libraries with more than 100,000 volumes are better off not taking inventory.

How Frequently Should Inventories Be Taken?

As previously noted, the inventory is the only method for calculating book loss that provides a complete list of the authors and titles of all missing volumes. In addition, it is the only method for calculating book loss that can be designed to perform a great many other jobs as well. (Its primary purpose, in fact, is to make the card catalog a reliable bibliographic tool.) There are disadvantages, however. Taking inventory is a massive effort, requiring that the library close for several days or that a portion of the staff occupy itself with the inventory for weeks or months. It is understandable, therefore, that the librarians at the Enoch Pratt Free Library, after a four-day inventory of more than 761,000 volumes, felt that inventories should not be taken more often than every 10 years.

Though the inventory is often intended to correct card catalog errors, it can also be used to weed, identify mislabeled books, etc. How often such corrections are necessary depends a great deal on the volume of loss the library sustains. One fairly quick way to determine that loss[21] is through sample techniques (discussed below). Whenever a sample indicates an intolerable loss, either overall or in a few subject fields, a full or partial inventory should be scheduled. The partial inventory, a full inventory of the sections most heavily used and, therefore, most heavily pilfered, is ideal. It deals directly with the problem loss area and is substantially less expensive than a full inventory.

What Will the Inventory Cost?

Item for item, the cost of taking inventory of library materials is low. Johns Hopkins University discovered that the cost per volume was four cents in 1969,[22] and the fully-automated University of Guelph estimated the cost per volume was slightly more than two cents in 1971.[23] However, the cost must also be measured against the replacement costs for volumes that will be discovered as lost and need to be repurchased. Many libraries suffering from budget crunches would not find an inventory of 1 million volumes (approximately $.02 x 1 million, or $20,000) "worthwhile" if they had to replace only 100 titles a year (approximately $15 x 100, or $1500).

The real cost of any inventory must be calculated in terms of library objectives and procedures. After objectives are defined and appropriate procedures are chosen, take the first 100 cards from the shelflist and calculate the time required for each step of the inventory. Multiply the cost for each step by the number of shelflist cards to be included in the inventory; then determine the number of man-hours required to accomplish each job. Multiply those by the hourly salary of the employees performing the task. Table II-1 provides examples of inventories conducted under various conditions, and their costs.

The following information, from a number of librarians who have taken inventories, may help to calculate costs:

- On an average, one person can process 63 books, not including pulling catalog cards, recataloging and double-checking the inventory, in an hour.[24] A more recent survey indicates that 42 books can be processed in an hour.[25]

- Two clerks with some professional assistance can inventory 100,000 volumes annually.[26]

- One person can withdraw 40 cards per hour from the catalog. Pulled cards can be checked for complete card sets at the rate of 1600 cards per hour.[27]

Table II-1. Examples of Inventories

Year	Institution	Volumes Inventoried	Library Closed	Library Open	Time Taken to Complete Inventory	Cost/Staff	Frequency
1951	University of Washington Libraries	600,000		X	1¾ years	440 clerical work hours for each month/5½ clerks	Continuous
1955	Enoch Pratt Free Library	761,041	X		4 days	10,468 man-hours; 5706 for actual inventory	Every 10 years
1962	East Chicago Public Library	145,000	X		8 days	Regular staff of 21, plus 16 temporary	Every 3 years
1969	Johns Hopkins University Library	1,300,000		X	10-13 years	$8000 a year 1 librarian and 2 clerks; librarian's salary not included in annual costs	
1971	University of Guelph Library	284,455		X	3 months	$4488 for computer time, $1826 a month for 8 student assistants	
1977	California State Polytechnic University Library	286,409	X		3 days	49 staff members, 27 student assistants	

THE SAMPLE

Sampling is a relatively efficient, inexpensive and quick method for determining the level of book loss. What it provides, if done properly, is an estimate of the actual number of books missing from a collection. One estimate, commonly used in statistics, is called the interval estimate. The interval is the range of losses that are most probable. After taking a sample and using the information it provides to compute an interval, statistical inferences about that interval's relationship to overall losses can be made. The process involved in making these inferences will be thoroughly outlined in the following pages. It begins with the sample, which provides data for constructing the interval; the final step, in which inferences are made about the intervals, results in a statement like the following: Library losses lie somewhere between 2.9% and 5.4%, with a 95% chance that this is the true range.

The section that follows contains some mathematical notation. The arithmetic is simple. By putting in real figures or estimates from their own experience, readers will find it surprisingly easy to learn how to make their own calculations of sample size and reliability.

How to Conduct a Sample

The first step is to determine what portion of the collection is to be sampled. Frequently serials and other special collections such as reference and rare books are eliminated, restricting the sample to circulating materials. Conversely, special parts of the collection, such as new acquisitions, are often sampled separately.

Gathering Data

If an educated estimate of loss is available, sample size can be determined prior to sampling. Since, however, that estimate is a guess and may necessitate recalculation, it is just as profitable to arbitrarily determine sample size. After so doing, the next step is to divide the collection size by the sample size, to determine which cards (volumes) will actually be sampled. For example, if the collection size is 100,000 and the sample size is 1000, every hundredth book will be sampled. Since 1 inch is the equivalent of 100 cards, taking one card every inch, rather than counting every hundredth card, will save time.

If the hundredth card is a reference book, a serial, or any item not included in the sample, the card should be eliminated. The total number of eliminated cards must be subtracted from the sample size to assure the accuracy of that number.

Using Data to Construct an Interval

The sample of every hundredth card provides an estimated percentage of losses. For instance, if in a sample of 1000 volumes 50 were missing, then the estimated percentage of losses would be 50 divided by 1000 or 5%. To make that percentage relevant to overall collection loss, however, it must be used to construct an interval. In the following equation, which should be used to construct an interval, p represents the estimate of loss based on sample data, z represents the level of confidence* to be placed on the constructed inter-

---

*Confidence levels determine the certainty with which one can make inferences about overall losses based on sample data. A few of the most frequently used values of z are as follows:

If a 68% level of confidence is desired z is 1.0.

If a 90% level of confidence is desired z is 1.64.

If a 95% level of confidence is desired z is 1.96 (rounded to 2.0).

If a 99.7% level of confidence is desired z is 3.0.

Most libraries are usually content with a 95% level of confidence.

val and σ is determined mathematically: $\sigma = \sqrt{\dfrac{\hat{p}\,(1-\hat{p})}{n}}.$

If sample data indicate a 5% loss and the sample size is 1000 then $\sigma = \sqrt{\dfrac{.05\,(.95)}{1000}}$

or .007 (when rounded). The equation for constructing an interval is $p - z\sigma < P < p + z\sigma$.

After level of confidence has been decided upon and data to establish an estimated percentage of loss have been gathered from the sample, solving the equation is a simple matter. If, continuing with the same example, a library sampled 1000 books, found 50 missing and desired to be 95% certain that the projected percentage of overall losses would lie within a specified range, the following formula would be used to determine that range:

$$p - z\sigma < P < p + z\sigma$$
$$.05 - 2\,(.007) < P < .05 + 2\,(.007)\ \sigma \text{ had been previously determined}$$
$$.036 < P < .064$$

This constructed interval indicates that the actual estimate of books missing from the entire collection is somewhere between 3.6% and 6.4%. There is only a 5% chance (with a 95% level of confidence) that the actual estimate of books missing from the entire collection is less than 3.6% or greater than 6.4%.

Narrowing the Interval

Some administrators might find an interval of 3.6% to 6.4% too large to be meaningful. Under some conditions, for example, a library might decide that it could tolerate a 4% loss, but a 6% loss would warrant some theft-prevention measures. What can be done in those situations? The interval can be narrowed by taking a larger sample. The following equation will determine how large the sample should be:

$$n = \frac{z^2\,p\,(1-p)}{e^2}$$

The equation should pose little difficulty, since most of its elements are now familiar. Small p is the estimate of loss provided by the sample; i.e., 5% if 50 out of a sample of 1000 books are missing. Small n is what the equation is being solved for—the new sample size. Small z is the confidence level, 1.96 (or 2.0 rounded), if 95% certainty is desired. The only unfamiliar element is e, which is simply the number that is added to or subtracted from p to construct an interval. (In a sense, e is the equivalent of $z\sigma$.) The library just picks a value for e that it has determined will provide a meaningful interval. If e is given the value of .005 (.5%), then the library has decided that only .5% will be accepted as a meaningful range.

To solve the equation, one need only insert the appropriate data. For example:

$$n = \frac{z^2\, p\, (1\text{-}p)}{e^2}$$

$$n = \frac{(2)^2\, .05\, (.95)}{.005^2}$$

$$n = \frac{.19}{.000025} = 7600$$

This means that if a library wishes to be 95% certain that the intervals it constructs from sample data will provide an estimate of loss that is no more than .005 (.5%) away from the actual percentage of missing books, then a sample size of 7600 books is necessary.

After sample size has been calculated and the sample is taken, the interval-constructing equation should be used to determine overall losses. For instance, if after taking the sample, 456 books are missing, then p is 6% (456/7600). This figure is plugged into the equation along with the confidence-level figure (1.96 or 2.0, if 95% confidence is desired). The calculation for σ which is $\sigma = \sqrt{\dfrac{p\,(1\text{-}p)}{n}}$ becomes in these circumstances

$$\sigma = \sqrt{\frac{.06\,(.94)}{7600}}\text{ or } .0027.$$

When all figures are placed in the equation, it reads as follows:

$$p - z\,\sigma < P < p + z\,\sigma.$$
$$.06\text{-}2\,(.0027) < P < .06 + 2\,(.0027)$$
$$.055 < P < .065$$

This means the library can be 95% certain that the actual estimate of books missing from the entire collection is somewhere between 5.5% and 6.5%.

Interval sampling will not provide the same kind of information as a book census or an inventory. A book census verifies the number of volumes physically present in the library; a sample will not. An inventory supplies bibliographic information for all materials missing from shelves; a sample does not. The sample is nevertheless an efficient, relatively inexpensive way to estimate the extent of collection loss.

Table II-2, appended to a 1972 Levittown (NY) Public Library report to the Council on Library Resources, calculates sample sizes. Note that as greater precision is required, sample size increases exponentially.

If annual acquisitions are being sampled and an estimate of loss is required to determine precise sample size, the following statistics may prove helpful:

- The 3M Company concludes that libraries annually lose 1%-3% of their collections.[28]

- A mean loss of 230 volumes a year in academic libraries at schools with an enrollment of 5000 or less is reported in Maxine H. Reneker's dissertation.[29]

- A 1975 survey of 79 academic libraries in Illinois indicated that average loss was 2.4%.[30]

- A 1974 survey of public, school and academic libraries in Vermont indicated a loss range of 5% to 5.9%. Higher losses were sustained by academic libraries.[31]

Table II-2.   Required Sample Sizes for Desired Precision at Expected Loss Rates with 95% Confidence*

Expected Loss Rate	Desired Limits	Sample Size
1% (.01)	±.2% (±.002)	9500
	±.5% (±.005)	1500
	±1% (±.01)	380
2% (.02)	±.2% (±.002)	18800
	±.5% (±.005)	3000
	±1% (±.01)	750
	±2% (±.02)	190
3% (.03)	±.5% (±.005)	4500
	±1% (±.01)	1100
	±2% (±.02)	280
	±3% (±.03)	125
5% (.05)	±.5% (±.005)	7300
	±1% (±.01)	1800
	±2% (±.02)	450
	±3% (±.03)	200
10% (.10)	±1% (±.01)	3500
	±2% (±.02)	860
	±3% (±.03)	380
	±5% (±.05)	150

*Reprinted by permission of Kenneth Kotnour, statistical consultant for the Levittown (NY) Public Library's study to determine the need for a book-theft-deterrent device.

Variations of the Sampling Process

If there is no way to gauge loss and there is concern about increasing the original sample size or taking too large a sample, libraries may plan a two-stage sampling procedure. In other words, they can take a sample to determine the sample size capable of producing the desired interval. In essence, the process is similar to that outlined above under "Narrowing the Interval," but with a different emphasis. In a two-stage sampling method the library plans on taking two steps instead of discovering that they are necessary. Miller and Sorum outline one such procedure applicable to sample sizes that are less than one-tenth of collection size.[32] They supply charts to determine initial sample size, then suggest that data from the initial sample be plugged into the equation for narrowing the interval.

Sampling techniques can be used very effectively in conjunction with measures for book loss. The most fruitful of these combinations are outlined below.

The Pilot Inventory

The estimated intervals of book loss provided by a random sample can be used to determine the necessity for a full or partial inventory. Random samples used this way are called pilot inventories. The point at which book loss seriously impairs the card catalog's public service value is an individual decision. Arlene Mangino, resources coordinator at the Montclair (NJ) Free Library, suggests that a loss rate of 8% or higher mandates consideration of inventory taking.[33]

In a 1967 pilot inventory of the Ohio State University Libraries, 5% was the arbitrary cut-off point.[34] Fortunately, their losses were less than 5%. The Houston Public Library was not so lucky: a 1974 random sample of that collection revealed losses of 41% with a plus-minus range of 3.5%.[35] What this meant was that two out of every five card sets were blind leads; a full inventory was mandatory. Although the full inventory of the Houston Public Library's main library took years, it began, logically enough, with those areas sustaining the highest losses. Those areas are easily identified from information collected during the sample. For instance, if three out of the 83 books sampled in the 200s are missing, then 3.6% of that collection is gone. While the Ohio State University Libraries did not plan a full inventory, they used the same logic to begin a series of partial inventories. Any areas of the collection with losses of 10% or higher were fully inventoried.

Both libraries demonstrated the effectiveness of using random sampling not only to calculate book loss, but to isolate those parts of the collection requiring greater attention. *The combination of the random sample and the inventory is a potent tool for collection control.*

Verifying Inventory Accuracy

In addition to determining the need for inventories, random samples can also be used to check the accuracy of inventories. When an inventory is completed, a random sample of shelflist cards is checked to assure both that a book has been inventoried and that it has been inventoried properly. While not an essential step, some administrators might want this extra proof of their inventory's efficiency and accuracy. The Houston Public Library performed such a test and discovered its inventory error was .007, one it could live with.[36]

Sampling Recent Acquisitions

Several libraries conduct a sample of the recent year's acquisitions to determine what percentage of their annual purchases are unavailable one or two years after purchase. While this estimate does not gauge overall collection loss, it provides a speedy estimate of the cost of most present library theft. In the early 1970s Lehigh University Library sampled one year's acquisitions and discovered 32% were missing in one year.[37] Book loss was costing one-third of its annual book budget. Regardless of other losses, Lehigh knew it could afford to devote up to one-third of its book budget to a theft-prevention program. That is the benefit of sampling recent acquisitions. The data supplied by such a sample indicate what theft-prevention and detection programs are within the library's budget.

Calculating Annual Losses

Since books other than those ordered in a given year are also subject to theft, a sample of a year's recent acquisitions will not provide a precise index to annual losses. In fact, no procedures already outlined will provide a precise annual loss rate, unless one takes an annual book census or an annual inventory. Because it is feasible for a large library to have lost one-quarter of its collection over a period of 100 years, but for the same library to sustain a current rate of loss of only 2%, the computation of annual loss rate is essential. Such a library would have to inventory to correct its catalogs, but it may not consider an annual 2% loss sufficient enough to warrant the extra cost of a theft-detection program. Realizing the importance of determining the annual loss rate, Michael Bommer of Clarkson College of Technology and Bernard Ford from the University of Pennsylvania Libraries have devised and tested two effective methods for its calculation.[38]

In the first method, which requires a one-year waiting period, a sample is taken, loss results are categorized by publication date, and the number of volumes in each category is determined. Charts will look something like the following:

Publication Date	No. of Cards	No. of Volumes	Items Missing
1966-1970	90	100	4

One year later, a second search is conducted. The difference between the previous and the current year's missing items is divided by the number of items in the sample. That percentage is applied to the estimated number of volumes in the library for each category.

The second method involves calculating the loss rate of a sample of recent acquisitions in relation to those items' circulation rate. The circulation rates of less recent acquisitions are then calculated and used to estimate loss rates in these categories, on the assumption that disappearance of materials is directly related to amount of use.

If a previous sample or inventory has pinpointed losses, Niland offers an alternate means of calculating annual losses.[39] The percent of loss between the first and second sample is adjusted so that the percentage of yearly loss reflects the number of volumes available each year and adds up to the figure for overall losses. At Washington University (St. Louis, MO), for example, 19,000 volumes disappeared over a 10-year period, representing an overall loss of 2.2%. Through trial and error, the library calculated that a loss of .3% compounded annually (applied to the book inventory of each year) would result in a total volume loss of 19,000 after 10 years.[40]

Effect of Misshelved Books

Materials that are misshelved or illegally borrowed on a temporary basis inflate book-loss calculations. Precisely to what degree is a matter of controversy. After a sample of 925 volumes at the University of Pennsylvania's Van Pelt Library in 1971, seven out of the 55 volumes presumed lost (13%) reappeared on library shelves one year later.[41] A few years later, the State University of New York at Stony Brook library released comparable figures: of the 30,000 volumes not located in the stacks during the three-year period when the library was converting its holdings to machine-readable form, about 13% were found upon a subsequent search.[42]

Other studies suggest even higher return rates. Of 40 missing books from a sample of 110,000 volumes at Northwestern University Library (Evanston, IL), 17 were found a year later.[43] Returns lowered overall loss from between 2.2% and 4% to 1.8%. In 1971 a sample of Washington University's central library indicated a collection loss of 5.5%. Ten months after the original search almost half of the missing volumes were located, and two years later only 2.2% were still missing. Sixty percent of the materials thought lost reappeared on shelves within approximately three years. The effect of returns on overall losses was staggering; that figure plummeted from 5.5% to about 2.2%.[44]

In view of such reports, three conclusions are possible. First, misshelved and temporarily missing materials do significantly affect book-loss calculations. Second, present statistics indicate that between 13% and 60% of materials supposedly missing may reappear on shelves within one and three years. Finally, libraries would be wise to study their own return rates before pricing security systems.

FINANCING THE INITIAL INVESTIGATION

Because most funding is awarded to libraries either for innovative projects relevant to the entire profession or for expansion of present resources, acquiring outside monies to deal with the problem of book theft and library security is no simple matter. Libraries are left on their own to combat the daily devastation to budget, service and staff morale resulting from theft. They have only two financial options for dealing with this problem: their own budgets and charity.

If the individual library must rely on its own resources to combat a suspected theft problem, how does it begin? First things first: the loss rate must be determined. As this chapter has demonstrated, a book census, inventory or sample will do that.

But who will pay for it?

If a book census is taken, costs will be cut by employing a reliable group of volunteers or Friends of the Library on a day or during a time period when the library is closed.

If an inventory is chosen as the best method for calculating loss, one way to reduce its cost is to close the library. In this way, inventory costs consist of only the usual expenditure for staff salaries. Book census costs could be absorbed in the same way.

If a sampling technique is chosen, obtaining assistance from the business or engineering department of a nearby college or university will reduce costs. Sampling the library collection is a perfect class project for beginning statistics students. As long as the project is closely supervised by the professor, such a cooperative venture is mutually beneficial. Students can test their theoretical knowledge in a practical situation and the library can learn if its book loss is significant. Such a cooperative arrangement is ideal for academic libraries, but other libraries should not hesitate to ask professors at nearby universities to participate in such a mutually beneficial undertaking.

Cost Justification for the Study

Presenting a brief but well-illustrated proposal to the officials in charge of the budget —the university provost for an academic library, the city manager or budget director for a public library—can help persuade these people that an inventory or census is a good investment.

Such a proposal should contain:

- a statement of the range of book losses experienced in comparable libraries,

- the cost of those losses in dollars and cents,

- the cost of those losses compared to the library's annual acquisition budget, and

- the way in which information from the study will be used to save money in the future.

Suppose a public library with 500,000 volumes wishes to conduct an inventory, and estimates that it can do the job for an out-of-pocket cost of $7500 by closing the library for a few days and using all the staff plus some temporary part-time employees.

The cost of the proposed inventory, $7500, should then be compared to possible losses from theft and other causes. If the library were losing 5% of its collection annually, for example, or 25,000 volumes, and half of those were books that should be replaced, the annual replacement cost would be $375,000, which is probably what a library of that size is spending on acquisitions.

Figure II-2 illustrates one way of presenting the relevant information in a concise form that is readily understood by those responsible for the library budget.

With a proposal in this form, spelling out all the relevant costs and the potential savings to be realized from better theft prevention, the library is well on its way to a complete cost-benefit analysis of theft-prevention alternatives. Electronic security systems are one of the most popular alternatives at present. (Chapter III includes a cost-benefit analysis of these systems.)

Figure II-2.   Summary of Proposal to Conduct an Inventory of a Library Collection

Purpose: To inventory the library's collections to determine how many volumes are missing, and in what areas, in order to recommend measures to save money in the future by reducing losses.

Cost: $7500 to be expended during the 1980-81 fiscal year.

This sum is composed of the following items:

Overtime for regular library staff	$ 3400
Part-time temporary workers	3000
Electricity and utilities for keeping library open during normally closed hours	200
Supplies	200
Contingency (10%)	680
Total cost	$ 7480
% of library budget request	.75

Benefits: The inventory will set a benchmark for the library's actual holdings. Periodic updatings by means of a census, sampling or a complete inventory will then measure annual loss rates and determine the advisability of various theft-prevention programs. The cost of different loss rates can be seen in the table below:

	Loss Rates as a % of Total Collection			
	1%	2%	5%	10%
No. volumes lost annually	5000	10,000	25,000	50,000
Replacement cost assuming one-half are replaced	$75,000	$150,000	$375,000	$750,000
Savings if loss rate is cut by 75%	$56,250	$112,500	$281,250	$562,500
Savings as % of annual acquisitions budget	15%	30%	75%	150%

Sources of Funds

Beyond the library's own budget, the institution may raise funds through appeals for outside donations by the community and/or business organizations. If charitable funds are solicited, publicity is essential. Local and school newspapers are usually supportive of such efforts, but the library must be careful, when devising its budget, to establish priorities. Communities cannot sustain repeated overtures for financial support.

Finally, there is the rare likelihood of a grant. Basic sources such as the *Foundation Directory* and the *Annual Register of Grant Support* should be consulted. Most foundations will not make grants for projects that are a routine part of an organization's activities, as library inventories ought to be. However, a library may be able to devise a plan that will yield significant research information of benefit to the wider library and educational community. In this way it might attract foundation support.

FOOTNOTES

1. "A New Kind of Inventory," *Library Journal*, May 1917, pp. 369-371.

2. Robert N. Sheridan, "Measuring Book Disappearance," *Library Journal*, September 1, 1974, p. 2041.

3. *Ibid.*

4. Joseph L. Wheeler and Herbert Goldhor, *Practical Administration of Public Libraries* (New York: Harper & Row, 1962), p. 476.

5. Margaret Monnelly, "Library Security in a High School: Is It Feasible?" *Moccasin Telegraph,* Winter 1978, p. 5.

6. Thomas L. Welch, "An Approach To an Inventory of the Collections," *Library Resources and Technical Services,* Winter 1977, p. 77.

7. Pamela Bluh, "A Study of an Inventory," *Library Resources and Technical Services,* Summer 1969, p. 367.

8. Bill Bolte, "Kentucky Librarians On Inventory," *Kentucky Library Association Bulletin,* Spring 1975, p. 15.

9. Catherine V. Von Schon, "Inventory by 'Computer,'" *College and Research Libraries*, March 1977, p. 147.

10. D.N. Banerjee, "Inventory Control," *Herald of Library Science,* January 1976, p. 36.

11. *Survey of Libraries in the United States,* v.4 (Chicago: American Library Association, 1927), pp. 130-131.

12. Timothy Walch, "The Improvement of Library Security," *College and Research Libraries,* March 1977, p. 102.

13. R.E. Beck and B.R. McKinnon, "Development of Methods and Time Standards for a Large Scale Library Inventory," in *Case Studies in Systems Analysis in a University Library,* Barton R. Burkhalter, ed. (Metuchen, NJ: Scarecrow Press, 1968), p. 55.

14. Robert S. Moore, "Missing Monographs in the Olin Library: A Preliminary Report," *Cornell University Library Bulletin,* October 1978, p. 1.

15. *Ibid.*

16. Chloe T. Sivertz, "Inventory Up to Date," *Wilson Library Bulletin,* September 1951, p. 69.

17. Vera Cunliffe, "Inventory of Monographs in a University Library," *Library Resources and Technical Services,* Winter 1977, p. 73.

18. Marian Sanner, "Pratt Takes Inventory," *Journal of Cataloging and Classification,* July 1955, p. 125.

19. Cunliffe, *op. cit.,* p. 75.

20. Von Schon, *op. cit.,* p. 151.

21. J.B. Clark, "An Approach to Collection Inventory," *College and Research Libraries,* September 1974, p. 343. Clark suggests that a 10% loss indicates the need for an inventory.

22. Bluh, *op. cit.,* p. 367.

23. Cunliffe, *op. cit.,* p. 75.

24. Hardin E. Smith, "Taking Inventory," *Library Journal,* September 1, 1962, p. 2848.

25. Clark, *op. cit.,* p. 351.

26. Bluh, *op. cit.,* p. 370.

27. Clark, *op. cit.,* p. 351.

28. Florine Fuller and Irene Glaus, "To Have or Not to Have a Security System," *Tennessee Librarian,* Spring 1974, p. 41.

29. *Ibid.*

30. Ted Kneebone, "Library Materials That Go AWOL or the Issue of Security in Illinois Academic Libraries," *Illinois Libraries,* May 1975, p. 341.

31. Jake Sherman, "Book Theft: How Bad a Problem for Vermont Libraries?" *Vermont Libraries,* September-October 1974, p. 18.

32. Bruce Miller and Marilyn Sorum, "A Two Stage Sampling Procedure for Estimating the Proportion of Lost Books in a Library," *The Journal of Academic Librarianship,* May 1977, p. 75.

33. Arlene Mangino, "Inventory: Luxury or Necessity?" *Wilson Library Bulletin,* March 1978, p. 574.

34. Irene A. Braden, "Pilot Inventory of Library Holdings," *American Library Association Bulletin,* October 1968, p. 1129.

35. Clark, *op. cit.,* p. 350.

36. Clark, *op. cit.,* p. 352.

37. Lehigh University Forum, Library Subcommittee of the Budget and Priorities, Planning and Resources Committee, "Synopsis of Professor Lindgren's statement in favor of his and Mr. Flato's motion of December 1972," (Bethlehem, PA: Lehigh University, 1972), p. 1.

38. Michael Bommer and Bernard Ford, "A Cost-Benefit Analysis for Determining the Value of an Electronic Security System," *College and Research Libraries,* July 1974, pp. 270-79.

39. Powell Niland and William H. Kurth, "Estimating Lost Volumes in a University Library Collection," *College and Research Libraries,* March 1976, p. 132.

40. *Ibid.* p. 132.

41. Bommer, *op. cit.,* p. 273.

42. Von Schon, *op. cit.,* p. 149.

43. Miller, *op. cit.,* p. 80.

44. Niland, *op. cit.* p. 130.

III

Theft Prevention Programs:
Electronic Security Systems

Widespread and successful use of electronic security systems have changed librarians' attitudes toward electronic surveillance. Initially skeptical, librarians asked whether such systems were necessary or suitable and whether they actually worked. They worked so well, in fact, that,the question became: Which system is best? Such a question assumes that electronic security systems provide the best protection and that one security system is better than another. Neither assumption is necessarily true. The question to ask is: *Which theft prevention program or system is most suitable to the type and magnitude of loss the library sustains?*

First a library must determine that on the basis of budget, annual losses, long-range goals and philosophy of service, an electronic security system is the most suitable program for its needs. The following review of the systems currently available should then help to identify the system that best fills those needs. Six questions are asked about each system:

- Who distributes it?
- How does it work?
- What does it cost?
- What will it protect?
- How is it installed?
- What are its special features?

Systems are discussed alphabetically by manufacturer or distributor in the following order:

Checkpoint Systems: Checkpoint Mark III
Gaylord: Gaylord/Magnavox
Knogo: Mark IV
LPS International: Stop-Loss

Sensormatic
Sentronic (Book-Mark)
3M: 1850, 1350, 1250

A final section outlines methods of cost-benefit analysis and major distinctions among the systems.

Before presenting details, however, we will note a few generalizations about the two basic types of systems, their safety aspects, their compatibility with automated circulations systems and the size of their detection area.

BYPASS AND FULL-CIRCULATING SYSTEMS

All electronic security systems operate in the same basic way. Treated targets are placed in library materials; when those materials are taken past sensing screens, strategically located by the circulation desk, the targets trigger an alarm. If a library book is properly charged out, however, no alarm will be triggered. There are two types of systems: bypass and full-circulating.

In a bypass system, materials charged out of the library are passed around the sensing screens of an electronic security system; they bypass the system. Such a system is less costly, but is not suitable in academic libraries, where students may leave and return several times a day with previously charged-out items. They are used most frequently in public libraries. Bypass detector tags are permanently sensitized.

Full-circulating systems accommodate libraries in which users frequently return with previously charged-out materials, such as school libraries. They are more costly because special units are required to deactivate and reactivate the targets placed in library materials.

SAFETY

Two health questions regarding the use of electronic surveillance equipment have been posed. Do the systems interfere with the operations of or endanger the users of pacemakers or hearing aids? Is the radiation they emit a danger? To answer the first question, most companies have submitted their equipment to testing. For instance, Checkpoint submitted the Mark II to extensive testing in late 1975 and early 1976 by the three largest American cardiac pacemaker manufacturers: Cordis Corporation (Miami, FL), Arco Medical Products Company (Leachburg, PA) and Medtronic, Inc. (Minneapolis, MN). All three indicated that Checkpoint did not interfere with the pacemakers they then manufactured.

In fact only one major incident involving electronic-security-system interference with cardiac pacemakers has ever been reported. In 1978 in England, a man using a pacemaker who had been doing library research and repeatedly exiting between the sensing screens of a 3M system, reported discomfort on one occasion. Tests were made to determine whether the electronic security system was responsible for the discomfort, but results were inconclusive. While the pacemaker in question, a fixed-rate pacemaker made by Joseph Lucas, Ltd., has not been manufactured for 20 years, 3M took the precaution of issuing a warning notice in 1979 (see Figure III-1). Approximately half of the 3M users elected to post it.

Figure III-1. Warning Notice to Users of Cardiac Pacemakers

Heart
Pacemakers

We have in this Library an electronically powered security system. It is entirely harmless under normal circumstances, but there is a possibility that it may affect a certain type of heart pacemaker.

If you have a pacemaker please contact a member of the Library staff before entering.

Hearing-aid interference seems to be even less of a problem. To date, the only reported inconvenience is the occurrence of a slight buzz audible to hearing-aid wearers as they exit between sensing units.[1]

If the library is concerned about either hearing-aid or pacemaker interference, patrons wearing either may be allowed to bypass the system. Another alternative is to turn the system off as such patrons exit between the sensing screens.

The question on radiation is more difficult to answer. In 1973 the United States Senate held hearings on the effects of low-level electromagnetic radiation (EMR) on the environment. Thereafter the Office of Telecommunication Policy directed an extensive research program on the matter. The results indicated that small amounts of EMR affected both behavior and the nervous system. Neither government interest prior to this investigation (P.L.90-602 on Electronic Product Radiation Safety), nor after it (1974 Radiation Control for Health and Safety Act), however, has altered the accepted United States standard for power density, which is 10mW/cm. square.

Most of the systems reviewed in this chapter use less than the maximum power allowed (Sentronic and Book-Mark, which operate on a magnetic principle, and Checkpoint, which operates on the principle of radio frequency, use none). Nevertheless, even those amounts exceed the standards of some European countries. As a result some of the systems listed are not marketable in those countries.

COMPATIBILITY WITH AUTOMATED CIRCULATION SYSTEMS

At present, practical field experience indicates that the installation of an electronic security system requires extra care when the library has or plans to acquire an automated circulation system. The basic problem is that radiation emitted from the circulation system's cathode-ray tubes (CRTs) may keep sensitized targets from triggering alarms. For instance, when the Biomedical Library at the University of California, Los Angeles installed a 3M Tattle-Tape system and a CLSI automated circulation system, the former was initially only 50% effective. The solution to the problem was relatively easy: sensing screens were moved farther away from CRTs. At the District of Columbia's Martin Luther King Memorial Library, 3M representatives suggested that book check units be at least three feet from CLSI CRTs.[2]

At the University of Texas at Dallas (UTD), discharging and desensitizing of library materials is part of the same automatic process. A patron inserts his ID in a card reader. If the borrower is in good standing, a message on a CRT will instruct him to place materials in a book tray, where a laser scanner reads the bar-coded label. If no reserves have been placed on the materials, the system desensitizes the detection strip. While library staff wrote specifications for the system, it was designed by Innovated Systems (Dallas, TX). The book theft detection system is a 3M model.

The system at UTD is fairly unusual. Only one principal automated circulation system vendor, Cincinnati Electronics, Inc., currently provides an interface between its system and an electronic security system (Checkpoint). Instead of shielding the Checklabel with a specially treated date due card (Checkcard), the automated circulation system's (CLASSIC) printer produces a specially treated date due receipt.

SIZE OF DETECTION AREA

In addition to systems' safety and compatibility with automated circulation systems, librarians have raised questions about the detection range of systems, the precise area in which sensitized materials may be picked up or detected by apparatus in the sensing columns. The smaller the sensing screens, the smaller the area of detection. The smallest screens, those of Gaylord and Sentronic, are 54 inches high and have a detection range of about 60 inches. The possibility of patrons exiting with books over their heads or pushed along with their feet should not present a problem to libraries with attendants at the circulation desk. Such behavior would be unusual, at the very least. If the desk is unattended, however, and patrons are aware that they can foil the system in these ways, a system with a greater detection area or a system capable of extending the detection area, such as Knogo and Sentronic, should be considered.

INTERFERENCE WITH ELECTRICAL OR ELECTRONIC DEVICES

Some librarians have been concerned that electromagnetic systems might interfere with the operation of such devices as computers, typewriters, calculators or electronic games. However, because the electromagnetic field created by these systems is present for only a short time, and because the energy is low-level, there is little chance of such interference.

What about watches? Being passed through sensing screens does not disturb watches; however, contact with activating or deactivating equipment can interfere with their operation. The 3M Corp. warns against inserting watches into the 940 book check unit. To prevent watches from becoming magnetized, Sentronic suggests that they not be worn in connection with the Sentronic system's activator.

CHECKPOINT SYSTEMS: CHECKPOINT MARK III

Who Sells It?

> Checkpoint Systems, Inc.
> 110 E. Gloucester Pike
> Barrington, NJ 08007
> 609/848-1800

Checkpoint Systems, Inc., formerly a subsidiary of Logistics Industries Corp., was spun off from that company in 1977 and is now independently owned. The company's sole business is the design and manufacture of electronic article surveillance equipment.

In the mid-1960s Peter Stern, an engineer at Logistics Industries Corp. and active member of the Cheltenham (PA) Free Library board, developed the Checkpoint Mark I book theft detection system. This first system, a metal detection bypass system, was installed and tested at several branches of the Free Library of Philadelphia in 1968. While the system was successful, there were numerous false alarms. In 1973 a system that effectively reduced false alarms was introduced. A bypass and full-circulating system, the Checkpoint Mark II operated on the principle of radio frequency.

In 1979 a third-generation system was introduced, the Checkpoint Mark III. Still operating on the principle of radio frequency, the Mark III is technically more sophisticated than the Mark II. It eliminates certain kinds of carry-through compromise (foiling the alarm mechanism by carrying materials through the sensing screens in a particular manner). The design and dimensions of the sensing screens also vary. Slightly smaller than the Mark II screens, which were clear plexiglas rectangles, the Mark III screens are chrome parallel loops.

In 1979 Checkpoint entered the retail market and devised a number of special targets and products for supermarkets, record stores and other retailers. One target, also applicable in libraries, is the Teeny Beeper, a standard part of the Mark III system. Considerably smaller than the Mark II Checklabel, the Teeny Beeper measures only 2 inches by 2 inches.

Although 63% of Checkpoint's sales in 1979 were to retail operations and 37% to libraries, Checkpoint has 1800 U.S. retail installations and more than 1500 U.S. library installations.

How Does It Work?

The way books are charged out in the Checkpoint system is different from the way books are charged out in other systems. Checkpoint's targets, whether Checklabels or Teeny Beepers, are always active. For this reason, a library staff member must either pass books around the sensing screens from behind the circulation desk or deactivate books by placing a specially treated date due card, called a Checkcard, over the Checklabel. If date due cards are not used, a small tab, called a Checktab, may be used to cover a Checklabel or Teeny Beeper. The tabs and Checkcards shield the Checklabel; they do not deactivate it. In all other full-circulating systems, targets are deactivated. One implication of this difference is that the Checkpoint system requires less equipment than the others. There are two basic equipment components in the Checkpoint system: sensing screens and an operator's control unit.

The overall dimensions of the sensing screens are 65 inches high, 12 inches wide and 3 1/4 inches thick (at the base of the screens). The upper portion of the screen is a loop or an arch of stainless-steel tubing. Called Quicksilver sensing screens, the Mark III screens are available in two colors: quicksilver and goldenrod. Their base, which houses the

Checkpoint Mark III sensing screens are chrome parallel loops. *Courtesy Checkpoint Systems, Inc.*

system's electronics, is cased with high-impact, shock-resistant, rigid plastic. The usual aisle width between screens is 36 inches. An unlimited number of sensing screens may be installed to protect large exit areas; each additional screen requires another turnstile or gate.

The operator's control unit is the system's power source. It is normally mounted behind or under the circulation desk. Included are an On/Off key switch; Power On indicator light; circuit-breaker reset button; and 10 feet of cord. It is 6 inches high, 5 inches wide and 3 inches deep and weighs 3 pounds.

In addition to a gate or turnstile, the system has one other feature of possible interest to librarians: a portable remote release. The release unlocks gates and turnstiles from locations as far as 75 feet from the actual system. Its use, however, entails the purchase of an additional control unit.

Of minor interest to librarians is Checkpoint's portable detector, a hand-held light-weight electronic scanner that a staff member holds near an individual to locate the concealed Checklabel that is causing the system's alarm to go off. It is 7 inches wide, 11 7/8 inches long and 1 1/4 inches deep, and it weighs 23 ounces. Its maximum detection range is 16 inches. When a Checklabel is detected, the scanner emits a muted audio signal. For the most part, the scanner is used in retail store installations.

System software includes Checklabels and Teeny Beepers, either of which come with holes in the center for application to cassette tapes and phonodiscs. Both have an adhesive film coating that requires no moisture, heat or other preparation prior to or after application. They are simply peeled off a sheet of release paper and applied. If they are part of a bypass system, the labels can be placed on the inside front or back cover, on any page, under a book jacket cover, under a bookplate, inside or under a bookpocket, or they can be printed and used as bookplates. In a full-circulating system the labels must be affixed under a bookpocket, inside a bookpocket (the Teeny Beeper fits easily) or on the back cover—i.e., in a place where they can be shielded by a Checkcard.

Checklabels measure 2 1/2 inches (plus or minus 1/10 inch) by 3 inches (plus or minus 1/10 inch) by 1/100 inch thick with adhesive coating. Teeny Beepers measure 2 inches by 2 inches by 1/100 inch thick with adhesive coating (see Figure III-2).

What Does It Cost?

Equipment

Systems	Quicksilver Single Aisle	$4400
	Quicksilver Dual Aisle	6600
Gates	Manual Entrance	450
	Electric Exit	550
Portable Verifier		500
Installation		250

Maintenance Service

There is an all-inclusive six-month warranty. A service contract is available in second and subsequent years for purchase and lease/purchase programs at a cost of 7% of equipment purchase value.

Terms

Net 30 days, F.O.B. Barrington, NJ 08007 (prepaid and billed on invoice). Prices exclude foreign import duties, federal, state or local taxes.

Lease/Purchase Plans

1. Two-year plan $280/month
2. Three-year plan   210/month
3. Five-year plan   154/month

Targets

	Quantity	Unit Cost	Printing: Add
Checklabels	500- 1,999*	$.30	—
	2,000- 4,999	.275	$.03
	5,000- 9,999	.25	.02
	10,000-14,999	.225	.015
	15,000-19,999	.205	.015
	20,000-29,999	.185	.01
	30,000-49,999	.17	.01
	50,000-99,999	.16	.01
	100,000-499,999	.155	.01
	500,000 +	.15	.01

*Minimum order for printing is 2500.

	Quantity	Unit Cost	Printing: Add
Teeny Beepers	1,000- 4,999	$.21	.03
	5,000- 9,999	.18	.02
	10,000-14,999	.15	.015
	15,000-19,999	.13	.015
	20,000-29,999	.11	.01
	30,000-49,999	.09	.01
	50,000-99,999	.08	.01
	100,000 +	.07	.01
Die Cutting	1,000-2,999*	$.03	(plus Checklabel cost)
for Cassette	3,000 +	.02	(plus Checklabel cost)
Tapes &			
Phonodiscs			

Replica	1,000- 9,999*	$.04	.025
Checklabels	10,000-19,999	.035	.015
(No Circuit)	20,000 +	.03	.01

Replica Teeny			
Beeper	1,000- 9,999*	$.03	.025
Checklabels	10,000-19,999	.025	.015
(No Circuit)	20,000 +	.02	.01

Checkcards   3″ x 5″ available in white, green, buff, cherry, blue, salmon.
Printed in Date Due Grid or 1/2/3/4:

	Unprinted	Printed (2) Sides
1,000 or more	$30/M	$35/M: White
	$35/M	$40/M: Color

Checktabs   1½″ x 2″ unprinted pressure sensitive on rolls: $8/M

Artwork Charge: $75 for initial printing orders.
Minimum quantity for ordering and shipping is 1000 of any mixed styles.

*Minimum order for printing is 2500.

What Will It Protect?

Checklabels can be applied to books, unbound periodicals, phonodiscs, phonodisc jackets, cassettes, cartridges, paintings, prints and reels of film if the hub is large enough. When affixed to unbound periodicals the Checklabel can be placed on the front cover with

Figure III-2. Actual Size of Checkpoint Targets

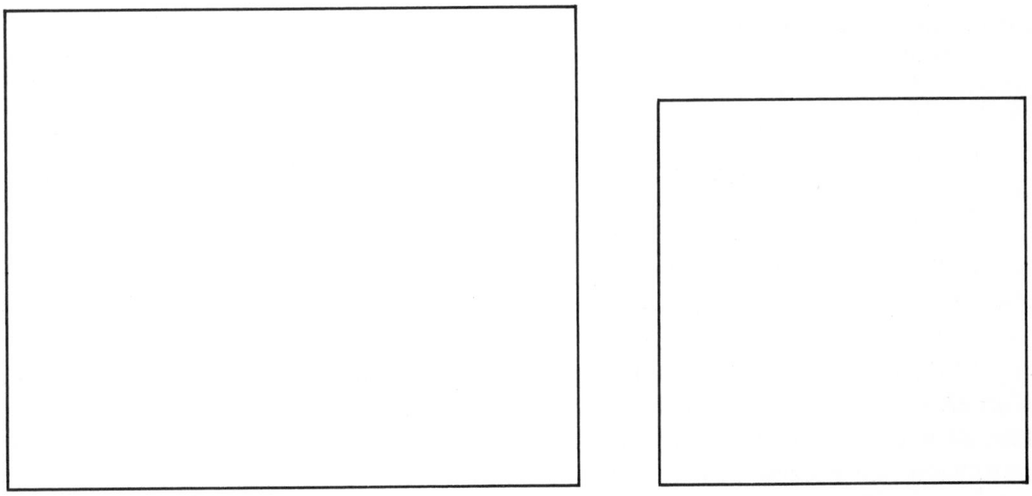

Checklabel

Teeny Beeper

a printed noncirculating sign, or it can be affixed to a subscription form inside the journal. If the latter technique is used the Checklabel can be saved and reused.

Checklabels cannot be placed on cassette cases; Teeny Beepers can.

How Is It Installed?

Installation entails anchoring the sensing screens, gates or turnstiles, and guide rails. The entire process can be completed in a few hours. The customer is responsible for supplying the 117-volt, 60-cycle AC convenience outlet near the location of the sensing screens. While the actual installation may be done by maintenance staff, Checkpoint personnel or outside contractors, Checkpoint employees supervise the process, make the final electrical connection and place the system in operation.

What Are the System's Special Features?

- The Checkpoint system is tailor-made for circulation systems using date due cards and/or bookpockets.

- Emitting no radiation, the Checkpoint system has no effect on pacemaker wearers, nor does radiation from CRTs interfere with its operation.

- User reports indicate that Checkpoint has the fewest false alarms and the least downtime.

- Checkpoint uses one target for both bypass and full-circulating systems; therefore conversion from one to the other is easy.

GAYLORD LIBRARY SYSTEMS: GAYLORD/MAGNAVOX

Who Sells It?

Gaylord Library Systems
Division of Gaylord Bros., Inc.
P.O. Box 4901
Syracuse, NY 13221
315/457-5070

Designed and manufactured by the well-known electronics and integrated circuitry company, Magnavox, and by a company with more than 80 years' experience in library supplies and furniture, Gaylord, the Gaylord/Magnavox Book Security System was first marketed in 1976. In June of that year, five systems were in use. One year later, there were 16 in public libraries, 15 in high schools and 13 in colleges. By early 1980, 90 Gaylord book security systems were installed and operating: 27 in public libraries, 36 in high schools, 24 in colleges and 3 in special libraries. Most librarians currently using the system were attracted to it because of Gaylord's record of service.

Since 1976 minor hardware changes have been made. Controls for gate/turnstile release and acoustical/visual alarm selection, which were previously a separate module, are now housed in the electronics module. In addition, the cut-out window area and decorative circles on the sensing screens have been removed to make their surfaces smoother. The biggest change, however, is the design of a second-generation system that uses a small full-circulating strip. The present system employs a 3 1/4-inch square target and 3/8-inch wide strips that come in 500-foot rolls. The new system will have small, pillar-shaped sensing screens and 3-inch by 1/4-inch full-circulating strips. It will also be less expensive than the first-generation system. A full introduction to the system is scheduled for the midwinter American Library Association (ALA) convention in February 1981.

Since specific information on the new system is unavailable until early 1981, the description that follows is that of the first-generation system.

How Does It Work?

The Gaylord/Magnavox Book Security System works on an electromagnetic principle. When library materials with a target are taken past sensing screens at the circulation desk, a physical, acoustical and visual alarm is triggered. A turnstile or gate locks, and either a muted acoustical sound is emitted or a light appears. When patrons leave, the sensing screens, by means of a small electronic field, search for a target.

Basically the system has three hardware components. A detection unit (two sensing screens) looks for concealed books; an electronics module provides power for all components and controls for resetting the system after an alarm; and a circulation unit (needed in full-circulating systems) deactivates and reactivates targets.

The two sensing screens that make up the detection unit are smaller than comparable units of other systems. Their standard height is 54 inches, standard width is 24 inches, and each screen is 5 5/8 inches thick. The aisle width is 28 inches. Screens are finished in Honeytone Teak Formica. Other Formica designs and colors are available, at additional cost.

The electronics module, which interprets signals received from the sensing screens, is the main power source for all the system's components. Since it activates the whole system, it is usually located on a shelf at the circulation desk. The system is ready for operation five minutes after the switch on the left front side of the module has been raised to the "up" position.

Two other controls are included in the electronics module. The first determines whether the alarm will be acoustical or visual. If a staff member switches the control to the right, the alarm will be visual; to the left, acoustical. The second control is a push button that resets the system. Depressing it turns alarms off, releases the turnstile or gate, and resets the system.

The circulation unit, which activates and deactivates targets in a full-circulating

Figure III-3. Actual Size of Gaylord/Magnavox Detector Tag

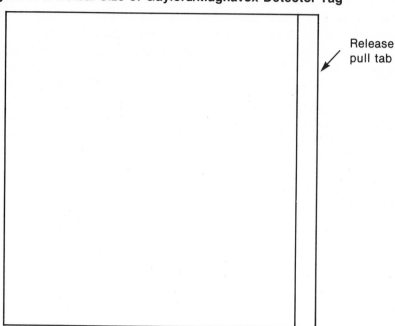

Release
pull tab

system, must be located at the circulation desk. It may either sit on the desk or be built in-to it, flush with the top. When books are being charged out—i.e., deactivated—the librarian pushes the switch down and wipes the book across the unit's top surface. When books are returned and the tags need to be activated, the librarian pushes the switch up and again wipes the book across the unit's top surface. When the unit is not being used the switch may be in the center or off position.

The Gaylord/Magnavox Book Security System uses the same tags for both its bypass and full-circulating systems. This makes conversion from one to the other easy. The tags are 3 1/4 inches by 3 1/4 inches by 3/200 inch thick and come with peel-off adhesive backings (see Figure III-3). They can be placed under book jackets, under bookpockets, inside bookpockets, or they can be used as printed bookplates. A special tool is needed to apply tags only if they are placed inside bookpockets; otherwise the release paper is remov-ed and the tag is applied. Two-inch pressure rollers, included in the initial tag shipment, can be used to assure smooth, uniform adhesion.

System components are illustrated in Figures III-4 through III-6.

In addition to 3 1/4-inch square targets, 3/8-inch-wide strips are available. Strips come in rolls of 500 feet. Like the square targets, strips have adhesive backs; unlike the square targets, however, they can be placed in gutters, spines and margins of books. Since the strip's length determines detectability, strips 4 inches or longer are recommended.

Figure III-4. Electronics Module and Circulation Unit, Gaylord/Magnavox Security System

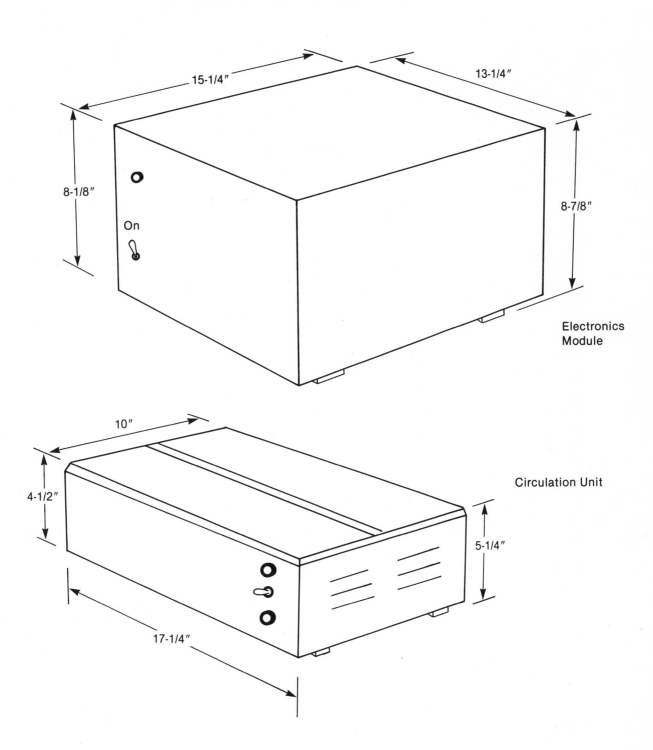

Electronics Module

Circulation Unit

Figure III-5. Interconnection Diagram, Gaylord/Magnavox Security System

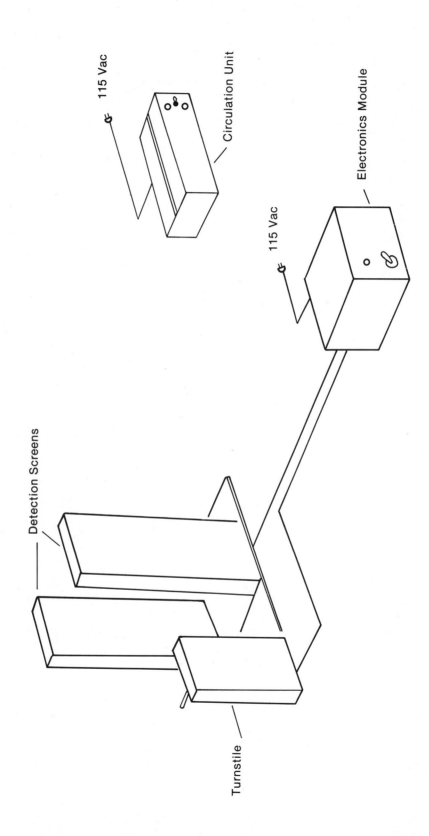

Figure III-6. Top View of Exit Aisle, Gaylord/Magnavox Detection Unit

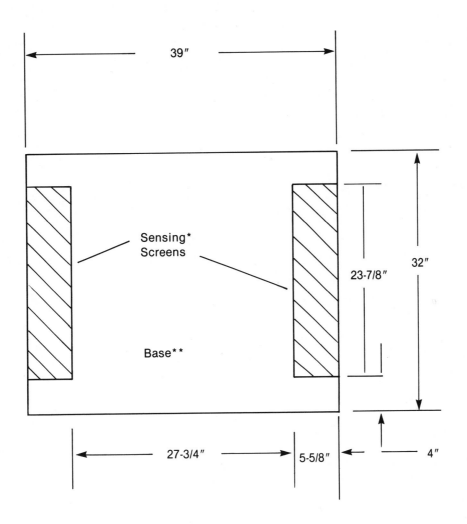

The carpet used to cover the base is 48 inches by 72 inches.

*The screens are 53-3/4 inches tall from the base; i.e., 54-3/4 inches from the floor.
**The base is 1 inch thick.

What Does It Cost?

Equipment

	Full-Circulating	Bypass
Detection Unit	$5055	$5055
Circulation Unit	675	—
Exit Turnstile or Gate	650	650
Entrance Turnstile or Gate	520	520
Installation	750	750
	7650	6975
Lease/Purchase Plan	$270/month	$241/month
Annual Service Contract After First 12 Months	$375	$375

With a Lease/Purchase Agreement, 60% of the payment may be applied to purchase at any time, and there is no charge for service. After 53 months, equipment will be owned.

Targets

Quantity	Unit Cost (Plain Targets)	Unit Cost (Printed Targets)
2,000*	$.16	$ —
5,000	.145	.16
10,000	.135	.15
25,000	.125	.135
50,000	.12	.13

One roll of strip material (3/8 inch by 500 feet) costs $60. The cost per inch is $.01.

*Minimum order for printing.

What Will It Protect?

The Gaylord/Magnavox detector tags can be affixed to books, unbound periodical issues, phonodisc jackets, cassettes, cartridges, paintings, prints, and reels of film. The tag is placed in the cartridge, cassette or film container. The only items that cannot be protected directly are phonodiscs.

The company recommends that magnetic tapes not come in contact with the circulation unit; if they do, loss of content may result. Magnetic tapes are not harmed if carried through the detection unit, however.

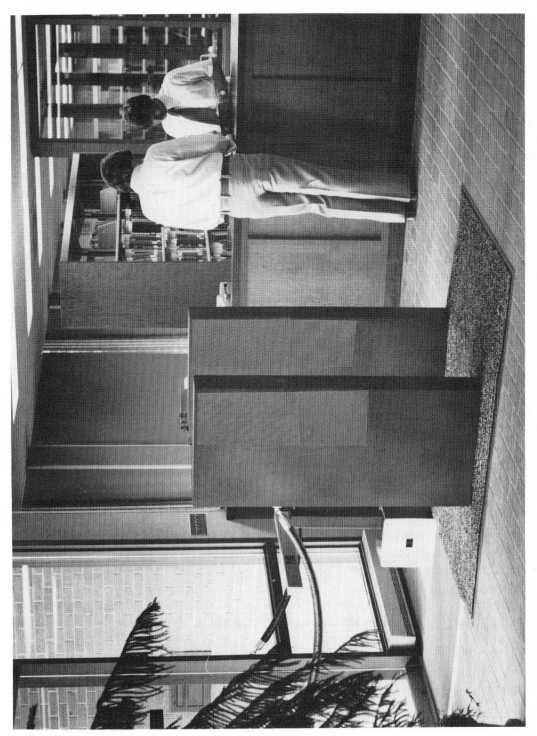

Gaylord/Magnavox sensing screens are smaller than comparable units of other systems. *Courtesy Gaylord Library Systems.*

How Is It Installed?

A mounting plate is used to install the sensing screens; this eliminates fastening screens to the floor. Because the mounting plate contains the wires that connect the two screens, no electrical conduit is required either in or on top of the floor. Therefore floor alterations are unnecessary. Both the mounting plates and ramps are covered with carpeting.

The library is responsible for providing outlets required for security system equipment. A standard 115-volt AC single-phase, 15-amp, dual receptacle properly wired with safety ground located within 6 feet of the sensing screens is essential, and is usually placed under the circulation desk. Full-circulating systems require an additional outlet for up to two circulation units.

What Are the System's Special Features?

- Gaylord/Magnavox uses one target for both bypass and full-circulating systems; therefore conversion from one to the other is easy.

- The circulation unit may be built flush with the circulation desk surface so that deactivation is simply a matter of sliding materials across the top of the circulation desk.

KNOGO: MARK IV

Who Sells It?

> Knogo Corp.
> 100 Tec St.
> Hicksville, NY 11801
> 516/822-4200

The Knogo Corp. was incorporated in New York in 1966 as the Monere Corp. and adopted its present name in August 1969. Knogo's sole business is the manufacture and leasing of article surveillance systems. At present it makes three. The first is a satellite system for stores with wide-open mall-type entrances; the second, a library system; the third, a patient control system that prevents senile and retarded patients wearing a special identification bracelet from either wandering from grounds or entering restricted areas. While libraries represent a small percentage of Knogo's sales—8% for the year ending February 28, 1979—the number of U.S. library installations continues to increase. In 1976 there were 10. By late 1977, 26 were in full operation and 10 more were being installed. In mid-1980 there were between 200 and 250.

For some time, litigation over the rights to Knogo's library system had been pending. 3M charged that its patents were infringed by Knogo, which denied the allegation and countersued 3M for antitrust violations. The matter has been settled out of court.

While still available, the Knogo Mark II system described in the first edition of *Book Theft and Library Security Systems* is no longer marketed actively. In its stead is a second-generation system, the Mark IV. There are both similarities and differences between the two systems. The choice of charge/discharge units remains the same; sensing screen design differs. The Mark IV sensing screens are smaller. A more important difference is the absence of a control panel to activate the system and control alarms. That absence lowers the system's cost and facilitates its installation.

In late 1980 Knogo announced plans to introduce a third-generation system, the Mark V, at the ALA 1981 midwinter meeting. The only change will be in the sensing screens, which will be "approximately shoulder height and three feet deep," according to a Knogo spokesman. Exact specifications and prices were unavailable at the time of this writing.

Knogo Mark II Book Detection System at Hicksville (NY) Public Library. *Courtesy Knogo Corp.*

How Does It Work?

The Knogo Book Detection System, available as a bypass or a full-circulating system, works on an electromagnetic principle. The company states that the system produces no harmful radiation and that no equipment emits microwave radiation.

When materials with targets are not properly charged out and are taken past the sensing screens, an audible alarm sounds and the turnstile or gate locks.

The system has two major hardware components other than gates or turnstiles: sensing screens and charge/discharge units. The two sensing screens, through which all patrons must exit, are 71 inches high, 36 inches wide and 6 inches thick; the width between them is 32 inches. While Mark IV screens are smaller than those for Mark II, which were 5 feet high and 5 feet wide, the detection range is greater: from ankle height to 70 inches, as opposed to the previous 60 inches. Screens are designed with a simulated wood-grain surface.

A library has three choices for charge/discharge units. The standard unit for full-circulating systems is the book verifier, a portable desklike console which activates and deactivates materials. It is 6 1/2 inches high, 14 inches wide and 15 inches deep. The librarian controls which function the machine performs by the use of a switch not accessible to patrons. It is called a verifier because, regardless of function, a red light on the front of the unit lights up (verifies) when a book with a sensitized tag is inserted.

The book check unit, like the book verifier, is a portable desklike console, measuring 6 1/2 inches by 14 inches by 15 inches, which activates and deactivates books. Again the librarian controls the function the unit performs with a switch which is not accessible to the patron. No verifying light is included, however.

The final charge/discharge unit is the universal unit. In addition to activating and deactivating books and journals, it also activates and deactivates phonograph records. It is rectangular and, unlike the other two units, its top surface is flat.

A master control panel, standard on the Mark II, is an option on the Mark IV. Should the library order one, it can be supplied with any of the following features:

- *Reset Button*—used to turn off audible alarm, open the turnstile or gate that is locked (upon alarm) and restore the system to its normal operating mode.

- *Audible Alarm*—an electronic solid-state tone-producing apparatus used to notify library personnel that the system has sensed the presence of a sensitized tape.

- *Volume Control*—to raise volume during peak noise periods such as when copiers are in frequent use, carpets are being vacuumed, and so on.

- *Duration Control*—controls duration of alarm tone.

- *Initiate Button*—to allow library personnel to lock gate or turnstile when desired.

Knogo book verifier.
Courtesy Knogo Corp.

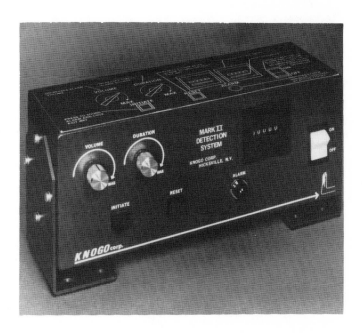

Knogo master control panel.
Courtesy Knogo Corp.

- *Alarm Light*—red light to signify alarm condition. It stays on until Reset Button is pushed.

- *Power On Light*—green light to show system is working.

- *Power Switch*— to permit turning off power to the electrically operated turnstiles or gates under emergency conditions.

- *Counter(s)*—a resettable digital readout showing number of patrons using library.

Another option is the wand or mass-target sensitizer, a small portable unit that sensitizes large numbers of books at one time.

In addition to hardware components, the Knogo Book Detection System has a versatile array of software. The standard target is 1/8 inch wide, 4 inches long and 1/100 inch thick, with rigid 3/8-inch-long tabs at the end (see Figure III-7). It is available in permanently sensitized form, for use in either bypass systems or special collections, or in sensitizable/desensitizable form, with 1/4-inch tabs. All targets come with adhesive backs protected by release paper. They are usually placed in the spines of thick books or on two randomly selected adjacent pages of a book or unbound periodical. However, they can also be put under hinges, within the boards of a book, under the bookplate and under the bookpocket. If inserted in spines, a 16-inch-long and 1/8-inch-wide wire is needed; otherwise targets are placed in a gutter, release paper is peeled off and pages are pressed against the adhesive.

Figure III-7. Actual Size of Knogo Detector Tag

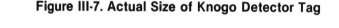

Special patent-pending semicircular targets for phonorecords and tape cassettes are 2 inches wide. Adhesive-coated, the crescent-shaped targets are placed between the label area and end groove of a record and are covered by a protective black label that makes detection or removal of a target difficult.

(Text continues on page 56.)

Knogo Mark IV sensing screens have greater detection range than those of the Mark II.
Courtesy Knogo Corp.

Knogo Mark V sensing screens to be introduced in 1981. *Courtesy Knogo Corp.*

Using the Knogo mass target or wand sensitizer. *Courtesy Knogo Corp.*

What Does it Cost?

Equipment

Equipment	Purchase	60-Month L/P	36-Month Rental (Min.)
Mark II Single Aisle	$5700	$140	$200
Mark II Dual Aisle	8000	195	280
Mark IV Single Aisle	5000	125	170
Mark IV Dual Aisle	7000	170	225
Gates	900	25	30
Turnstiles	1100	30	35
Charge/Discharge Verifier	1450	40	50
Charge/Discharge	1000	25	40
Desensitizer	300	10	15
Wand Sensitizer	Priced On Special Order		
Installation			
Single Aisle (with accessories)	$400		
Dual Aisle (with accessories)	700		

A 90-day warranty covers all electronics.

Cost of annual service contracts:

Single Aisle System	$350
Dual Aisle System	500
Charge/Discharge	60
Charge/Discharge with Verifier	60
Gates	50
Turnstiles	50

Targets

Quantity	Unit Cost
1,000- 4,999*	$.10
5,000- 9,999	.095
10,000-24,999	.09
25,000-49,999	.085
50,000-99,999	.08
100,000 +	.075

Record and Cassette Strips: $.30 on all quantities.

*Minimum order for printing.

What Will It Protect?

The Knogo system's tags can be affixed to books, unbound periodicals, phonodiscs, phonodisc jackets, cassettes, cartridges, paintings, prints, reels of film, calculators, typewriters, pictures and art pieces. Magnetic tapes will be wiped clean if they are deactivated, but will suffer no damage if walked through the sensing unit.

How Is It Installed?

Installation is handled by Knogo personnel. Normally only two to three days are necessary; this includes fine tuning. It is the library's responsibility to furnish a 110-to-120V, 60Hz dedicated line for the sensing unit (with nothing else on that line) and regular outlets for other equipment.

What Are the System's Special Features?

- Special crescent-shaped targets can be applied directly to phonorecords and tape cassettes.

- At present Knogo has one of the smaller detection strips.

- Large numbers of books can be sensitized at one time with the mass-target sensitizer.

LPS INTERNATIONAL: STOP-LOSS

Who Sells It?

> Loss Prevention Systems
> LPS International, Ltd.
> 2775 Curtis Drive
> Smyrna, GA 30080
> 404/432-0010

LPS International owns the original patents that the 3M Tattle-Tape system is licensed to use. Only a few systems have been produced in Europe, where they are marketed under the name Stop-Loss.

In the U.S., LPS is stressing retail applications for its system. It hopes to conclude an agreement whereby a company specializing in the library field will distribute Stop-Loss to libraries. However, to date it has not reached such an agreement. LPS claimed to have 12 orders from libraries at the end of 1977 and several installations in 1980, but as the company would not reveal the names of any customers, this statement could not be verified. Information on costs was also unavailable.

In the absence of any installations in the field, the specifications, released by LPS and detailed below should be carefully verified by any library considering the system.

How Does It Work?

LPS, available as a bypass or full-circulating system, operates on the electromagnetic principle. An encoded paper-thin label is attached to library materials. When materials are carried through a control area without being checked out properly, an alarm is triggered. The interrogator and detector cabinet, exit control panels and de-reactivator are the system's major components. The system employs electronic logic to monitor signals in order to avoid triggering false alarms.

The interrogator and detector cabinet is the system's power supply. The unit is 19 1/2 inches high, 20 inches long and 15 3/4 inches wide. The design of LPS exit control units is highly flexible. If a floor plan is submitted to the LPS Engineering Department, a design can be constructed to fit any desired requirements. The commercial units usually measure 5 feet, 6½ inches high, tapering to 2 feet, 10½ inches high by 5 feet long by 2 3/4 inches wide. The company would not provide exact dimensions for library units.

The manual de-reactivator, for use in full-circulating systems, activates and deactivates the LPS detector tag. The unit measures 1 foot, 4 3/8 inches high, 1 foot, 6 1/2 inches long and 1 foot, 1 3/4 inches wide. It weighs 30 pounds and its opening measures 4 5/8 inches high, 13 3/4 inches long and 10 1/2 inches wide.

The LPS system uses two kinds of targets (sensors). One-way tags are permanently sensitized. (The tags are removed in the retail industry when a protected item is sold.) They are the basis of protection for noncirculating materials such as reference books as well as for all materials in a bypass system. Two-way targets, shipped in an active state, are used in full-circulating systems.

Targets are 2 inches long and 1/8 inch wide. They can be applied with adhesive, staples and pins, or through sewing and heat sealing. Libraries would be most likely to use adhesive-backed sensors. Those pieces could be placed in book covers and book spines or they could be printed as labels. No special tools are needed to insert targets. LPS also makes targets that are 7 inches long; special tools must be used to insert these strips (see Figure III-8).

What Will It Protect?

LPS detector tags can be affixed to books, unbound periodicals, phonodiscs, phonodisc jackets, cassettes, cartridges, paintings, prints, reels of film, furnishings and manuscripts. Tapes should not be passed through the de-reactivator unit.

Figure III-8. Actual Size of LPS Detector Target and Strip

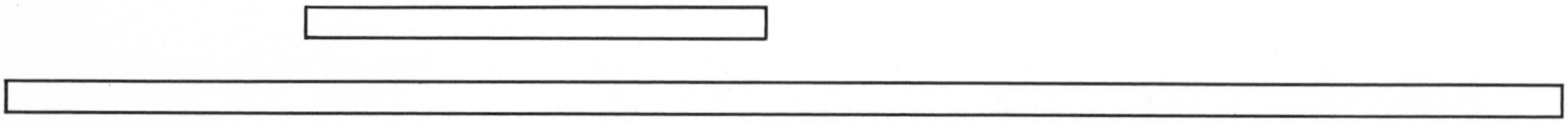

How Is It Installed?

The following electrical requirements are necessary:

- 115 volts, 60 cycles, 8 amps

Also available:

- 220 volts, 60 cycles, 4 amps or
- 220 volts, 50 cycles, 4 amps

What Are the System's Special Features?

- One detector tag is extremely small, only 2 inches long.

- The company claims that use of electronic logic in the system eliminates the triggering of false alarms.

SENSORMATIC

Sensormatic
500 NW 12th Ave.
Deerfield Beach, FL 33441
305/427-9700

In the late 1960s and early 1970s, Sensormatic, now the leading retail electronic security system vendor, installed systems in two libraries: Prince George's Community College (Largo, MD) and Santa Ana Public Library (Santa Ana, CA). Called sensors, targets were oblong, approximately 1 1/2 inches by 1/2 inch, with adhesive on one side. Similar to Checkpoint targets, they were "detuned" by means of special date due cards. While staff at both libraries were satisfied with the system's performance, they were unhappy about the difficulty of obtaining supplies for it. The system at Prince George's Community College has been replaced by a Checkpoint Mark III.

Both installations are of historical interest only. Of much greater consequence is Sensormatic's Florida test of a new library system, magnetic in principle, started in the fall of 1980. Sensormatic hopes to eliminate the frequent false alarms usually associated with magnetic systems. If the test installation is successful, another library security system may be on the market.

SENTRONIC (Book-Mark)

Who Sells It?

> Sentronic International
> Division of General Nucleonics, Inc.
> P.O. Box 116
> Brunswick, OH 44212
> 216/225-3029

Founded in 1961, Sentronic International designs and manufactures security systems for use in industrial and institutional operations. In 1963 it developed the first theft-detection system on the market. In 1964 that system was installed in the Grand Rapids (MI) Public Library. By 1976 more than 200 Sentronic systems were in use; more than 80 were in libraries.

In 1971 the Library Bureau of Herkimer, NY, became a licensee, distributing a variation of the Sentronic Library Security System called Book-Mark, which was installed in the Mohawk Valley College Library (Utica, NY), the Knoxville-Knox County Public Library (Knoxville, TN), the Ohio College of Podiatric Medicine Library (Cleveland, OH), the City of Inglewood Public Library (Inglewood, CA) and others. In 1977 the Book-Mark system was acquired by General Nucleonics. From that point on, changes made in Sentronic were incorporated into Book-Mark. One such change, presently in the offing, is the option of gates. In the past the Sentronic system was available with turnstiles only.

While Sentronic is willing to modify Book-Mark units, it markets Sentronic only. That product has undergone its own changes. For example, a previous Sentronic option was the Scanscope feature, which pinpointed the exact location of a concealed or shielded theft. Today's basic model, the S-64, omits the Scanscope feature, uses slightly smaller targets and has a different sensing screen design. There were at least 100 systems, including previous Book-Mark installations, in libraries as of 1980.

How Does It Work?

Unlike other electronic security systems which use electromagnetic or microwave radiation, Sentronic employs magnetism as an energy form. In other systems patrons are surveyed or interrogated by radiation whenever they pass by sensing screens at the library's exit passageways. In those systems targets cause an alarm, but the system is on whether or not they are present.

In magnetic systems, however, it is only the presence of an active target that triggers interrogation.

In other respects Sentronic, a full-circulating security system with bypass possibilities, operates much the same as other systems. Sentrons, magnetic targets placed in library materials, produce an alarm if materials are not deactivated before being taken past sensors in exit columns. The alarm is visual, audible and physical (the turnstile locks).

The sensing system consists of small probes, 3/8 inch in diameter and 3 inches long, that can be concealed in door jambs, wood frames, aluminum columns or molded plastic components to any height desired. A standard sensing system, however, is mounted within two aluminum columns on a metal base plate in conjunction with a turnstile or gate. Once tapering from a base of 12 inches by 5 1/2 inches to 6 inches by 4 inches, screens are now 54 inches high, 3 inches wide and 5 inches deep. The width between columns is 28 inches. Promised detection ability is not less than 60 inches high by 36 inches wide by 12 inches deep; special finishes are available at extra cost. A control console is connected to the system by means of a cable, which can be concealed.

A hexagonal unit with an aluminum cabinet and rigid urethane molded side panels measuring 8 inches by 16 inches by 12 inches, the control console contains the power supply for the system and the electronics for producing alarms and resetting the system after alarms. It contains an on/off switch, a sensitivity adjust, a volume control, a reset button and an electric counter, when required.

Sentronic charge/discharge units may be either portable or permanent. Most equipment is permanent; however, one model activator is portable. The portable activator is an

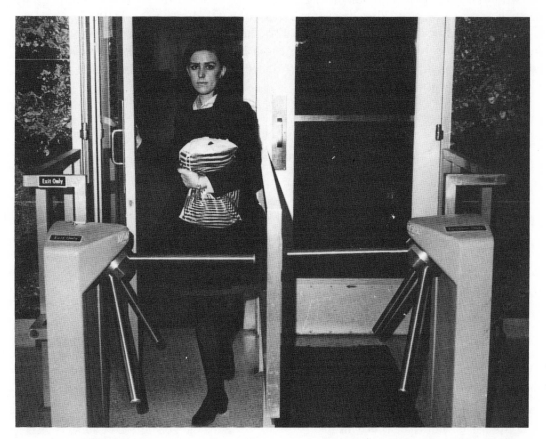

The Sentronic sensing system is concealed within the door jambs of the exiting door.
Courtesy Sentronic International.

automatic piece of equipment; that is, it performs only one function. It is mounted on a wheeled table, measures 2 feet by 2 feet, 2 inches by 2 feet, 6 inches, and is comprised of an on/off switch, indicator lights and an 8-foot electric cord and plug.

Other automatic units are permanent. The automatic activator is mounted in the book-return chute. It measures 11 inches by 20 inches by 5 1/2 inches with a 4-inch by 13 3/4-inch opening. When books are returned through the chute they are automatically activated. That unit's counterpart, the automatic deactivator, whose dimensions are 14 inches by 14 inches by 4 inches, is operated a little differently. When library materials are checked out, a library staff member presses a foot switch and slides books over the circulation counter. The deactivator is concealed under this counter (see Figure III-9).

In addition to these components, a hand probe is available for use with model S-64. The hand probe detects the source of alarm. Sentronic's plans include making available a discriminator, an automatic feature which will identify the particular field emitted by a sentron instead of a foreign magnetic field by some object that might have been magnetized accidentally or intentionally by a patron.

System software accommodates books, periodicals and audiovisual materials. There are two kinds of targets for books (see Figure III-10). The ST75 has permanent pressure-sensitive adhesive on two sides, measures 2 inches by 3 1/4 inches by 1/100 inch and may be placed behind bookpockets, bookplates and endpapers or concealed during rebinding. The ST74 is a strip for use with periodicals as well as books. Measuring 1/4 inch by 7 inches by 1/100 inch, the ST74 also has permanent pressure-sensitive adhesive on both sides. It is applied to gutters or spines.

Figure III-9. Sentronic Activator/Deactivator

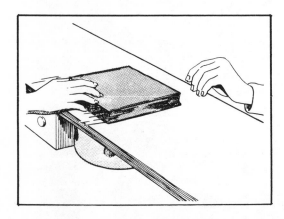

Books being automatically deactivated during normal charge-out function at circulation desk.

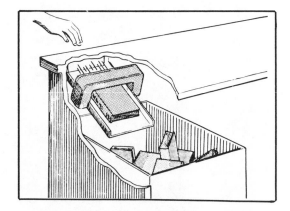

Books are energized or activated when initially treated or following their return to the library by patron.

Figure III-10. Actual Size of Sentronic Detection Targets

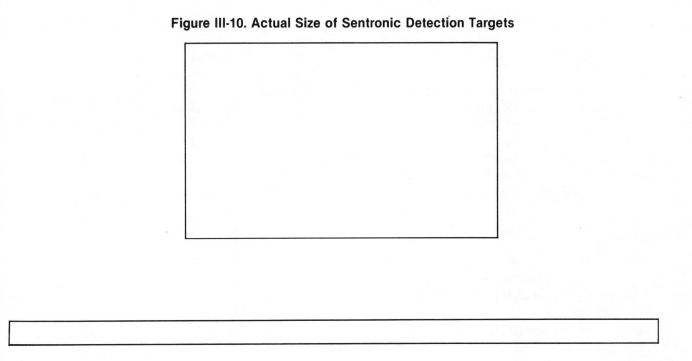

Targets for cassettes and tape decks are thin labels with one pressure-sensitive adhesive side for application on the actual tape (see Figure III-11). Targets for phonodiscs are circular label-like targets with adhesive on one side. One is for 33 1/3-RPM records; the other is for 45-RPM records. Special target types and sizes can be made to order for any application.

Figure III-11. Sentronic Targets for Cassettes and Tape Decks

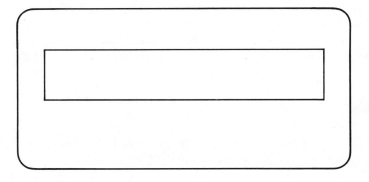

What Does It Cost?

Equipment

Sensing Columns, Metal Base, and Control Console Charge/Discharge Units	$5500
Portable Automatic Activator	925
Automatic Activator, mounted in book return	895
Automatic Deactivator	895
Hand Probe	350
Turnstile	595
Gate	625
Six-digit Electronic Counter	195
Five/six Digit Mechanical Counter	97.50
Special Finishes	49.50 and up

The warranty for Sentronic is one year.

Targets

	Unit Cost
Books (ST75)	$.10
Periodicals (ST74)	.10
Tape Cassettes (ST73)	.25
Phonodiscs, 33 1/3 RPM (ST72)	.25
Phonodiscs, 45 RPM (ST71)	.25
Tape Decks (ST70)	.25

What Will It Protect?

Sentronic detector tags can be used to protect books, unbound periodicals, phonodiscs, phonodisc jackets, audio and video cassettes, cartridges, paintings, prints, reels of film and EDP materials. No targets are needed to magnetize office equipment, hand tools, typewriters and other equipment that incorporates some ferromagnetic material susceptible to a magnetic charge. Magnetic tapes may be activated and deactivated without being damaged.

How Is It Installed?

Sensing screens are mounted on a rigid but portable base. Sensing units and charge/discharge units each require either a 110V/60 or a 220V/50 outlet.

What Are the System's Special Features?

- Automatic charge/discharge units are available.

- There are a variety of targets, some especially designed for phonodiscs and cassettes.

- The hand probe will pinpoint the location of concealed materials.

- The Sentronic system emits no radiation and is safe for pacemaker and hearing aid wearers.

The Sentronic system has locking turnstiles. *Courtesy Sentronic International.*

3M: 1850, 1350, 1250

Who Sells It?

> 3M
> Library Systems, 220-9E
> 3M Center
> St. Paul, MN 55144
> 612/733-2851

3M is a major corporation, with subsidiaries in 49 foreign countries, and 94 plants and 122 sales offices in the United States. Products and services are diverse. There are abrasives, adhesives, building service products and chemicals, graphic systems, advertising services, protective products, recording materials, photographic printing, industrial graphics and nuclear products, and health care services and products. Electronic article surveillance systems were introduced to libraries in 1970, then to bookstores in 1979. The bookstore market represents only a small percentage of sales.

Since 1977 3M has changed the name of its hardware and software, introduced a target for cassettes, introduced a new model, and modified the sensing screen dimensions and control panel design of previous models. Once referred to as the Tattle-Tape and the Spartan, the largest and smallest 3M systems are now called the 1850 and the 1250. The 1350, a medium-priced sensing unit, was introduced in 1980. Tattle-Tape Detection Strips, once called either single (SS) or dual (DS) status, are currently referred to as permanently sensitized or programmable. For instance, the sensing screens of the 1850 are 2 5/8 inches narrower than those of its predecessor, the Tattle-Tape Book Detection System.

As of 1980, more than 3000 3M theft-detection systems were installed in libraries throughout the world.

How Does It Work?

Either bypass or full-circulating 3M systems are available. They operate on an electro-magnetic principle. A low-frequency electrical signal is triggered when a thin metallic strip is stimulated by an alternating electromagnetic field. If a patron attempts to pass through the sensing unit with materials that have not been checked out properly, an alarm sounds and the gate locks.

There are three models available, the 1850, 1350 and 1250. While all systems have the same hardware components—sensing screens, charge/discharge units and exit/entrance gates or turnstiles—sensing unit dimensions and designs vary. The 1850, for example, consists of a lattice, a column housing the detector, a heavy-duty aluminum base plate and a carpet. The installed lattice is 77 inches high. The base is 8 3/4 inches thick and 59 inches long. The detector post is 56 inches high and 9 1/4 inches square. A traffic meter to count the number of people exiting the system is located in the base of the lattice. For heavy-traffic areas, there is a dual corridor version, the 1850-2, which includes two base plates, two carpets, two detector posts and one lattice, positioned between the two posts.

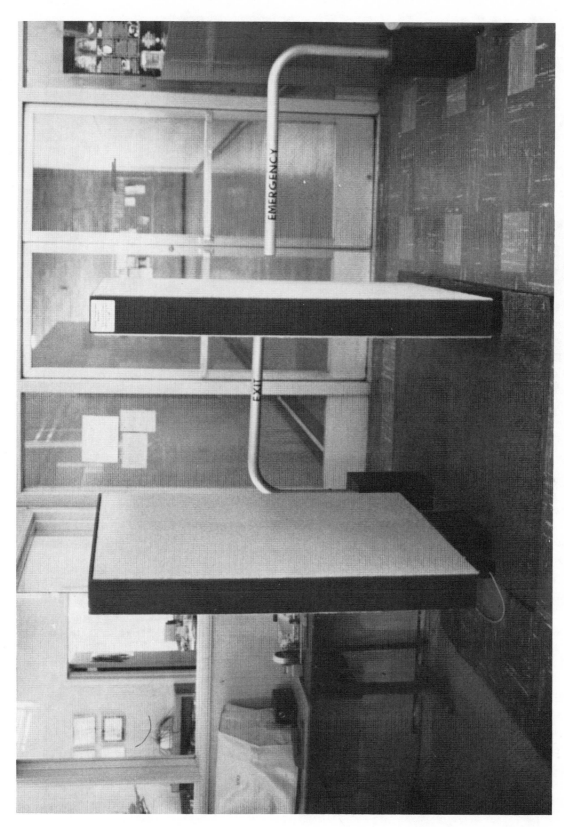

The sensing unit of 3M's 1250 has two panels. *Courtesy 3M.*

3M's 1850 sensing lattice, detector column, carpets and base plates. *Courtesy 3M.*

3M's 1350 includes two open lattices, aluminum base plates and carpet. *Courtesy 3M.*

The 1350 includes two open lattices, each measuring 64 inches high, 4 1/2 inches thick and 38 1/8 inches wide. The sensing unit of the 1250 has two panels; their dimensions are the same as those of the 1350. Both the 1350 and 1250 include aluminum base plates and carpets. The aisle width in all systems is 32 inches.

Compatible with all three sensing units are two sensitizing/desensitizing units: the 950 and the 940. Both desensitize targets so that properly checked-out materials can be carried through the sensing unit, and both also resensitize returned items so that they are once more protected by the system. The 950 is 20 inches long, 18 1/2 inches wide and 6 1/2 inches deep. A signal light to the left indicates whether the strip is sensitive or nonsensitive. To activate or deactivate library materials, a staff member pushes the switch, setting the unit to perform only one of these functions. Then the staff member slides the book through the unit, with the book's spine against the unit. An audible thump means the machine has performed the desired task. The 940 is 16 3/4 inches long by 5 3/4 inches high by 5 1/4 inches deep, and weighs 15 pounds. As with the 950, one switch controls the sensitizing or desensitizing process. A staff member sets the switch to the proper function, inserts library material into the "tunnel" opening and moves material to the left. While less expensive and more portable than the 950, the 940 does not indicate whether materials are sensitized and does not accommodate materials wider than 10 inches or thicker than 2 3/8 inches.

There are also circulation-desk control switches that perform the following functions:

- alarm activation
- gate-unlock mechanism
- stand-by switch

Two kinds of strips are available for use with the 3M systems: permanently sensitized and programmable (see Figure III-12). Permanently sensitized strips cannot be desensitized and are used in noncirculating or bypass applications. Programmable strips are used for full-circulating applications. Both are available with adhesive on one or both sides of the strip. Strips with adhesive on one side are designed specifically for insertion in the spine of a book, using a thin metal tool. Strips with adhesive on both sides are designed for placement between the pages of periodicals, paperbacks and other materials not suitable for spinal insertion. The strip is aligned in the book's or unbound periodical's gutter, the extended liner is removed and the pages are pressed against the adhesive. If desired, a special unit, the 810 Book Holder, facilitates stripping by holding books in the proper position.

Permanently sensitized cassette labels, which come six to a sheet in boxes of 300, are also easy to apply. Each box includes a guide, a small device that fits into the holes of a cassette to assure accurate label placement. Labels are peeled off release paper, placed over the guide and pressed onto the cassette.

Programmable strips are 6 1/2 inches long, 3/16 inch wide and .014 inch thick with one adhesive side, .007 inch thick with both adhesive sides. Permanently sensitized strips are 6 1/2 inches long, .125 inch wide and .012 inch thick with one adhesive side, .005 inch thick with both adhesive sides. Cassette labels measure 3 1/2 inches in length, 9/16 inch in height and have rounded rectangular windows 2 6/16 inches long by 6/16 inch wide.

3M's 940 sensitizing/desensitizing unit. *Courtesy 3M.*

Figure III-12. 3M Detector Strips

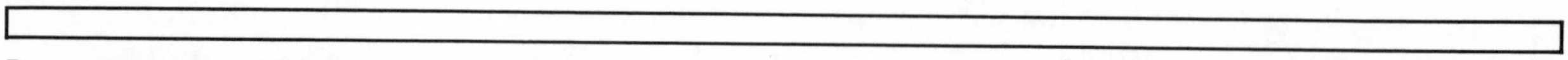

Permanently sensitized strip

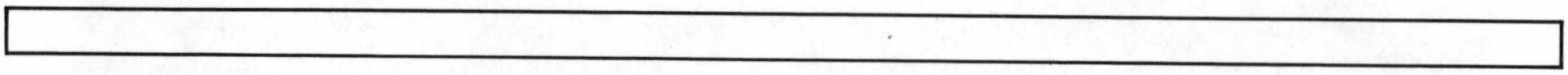

Programmable strip

What Does It Cost?

Equipment

	Unit Cost	Yearly Maintenance
1250	$3600	$270
1350	4600	270
1850	5475	420
1850-2	6900	550

Sensitizer/Desensitizer

	Unit Cost
950	$1315*
940	525*
Gates	$450-950†
810 Book Holder	175
Installation	439

*Included in system maintenance.
†Price includes GMA.
There is a 90-day warranty.

Targets

(1,000 per box)	Programmable	Permanently Sensitized
1,000	$.155	$.125
2,000-7,000	.135	.110
8,000-15,000	.115	.100
16,000-25,000	.110	.090
50,000 +	Prices quoted upon request	

Cassette labels are $90 for a box of 300.

The 3M theft-detection systems may be leased, purchased outright or purchased on an installment basis. Leasing and installment-payment plans are available for one- to five-year periods. Rates lower than commercial ones are available to any governmental unit, including the state, city, county or township; educational, administrative or school system; the police and fire departments; and the like. These rates are available upon request.

What Will It Protect?

3M detection systems protect books, unbound periodicals, records, record jackets, cassettes, paintings, prints, films, pictures, certain artifacts, manuscripts and so on. Magnetic tapes must be passed around the sensing units, since they cannot be put in the sensitizers/desensitizers.

How Is It Installed?

For an additional cost, 3M will provide a technician to properly install and adjust the system. Usually installation can be done in one day. Since systems are mounted on aluminum plates, no floor drilling is necessary to anchor sensing screens.

The library must provide the following electrical circuits:

- a dedicated grounded electrical line providing 110V, 60Hz power for the sensing units

- a 110-120V AC outlet for each sensitizer/desensitizer

- a 110-120V AC outlet for remote entrance gates.

COST-BENEFIT ANALYSIS FOR SECURITY SYSTEMS

The decision to buy an electronic security system or one of the alternatives discussed in Chapter VI, eventually comes down to hard economics. Convinced of neither the effectiveness nor the cost-effectiveness of electronic surveillance equipment, Matt Roberts estimated in 1975 that a new library with 50,000 volumes, which added 50,000 volumes each year, would pay an average annual cost of $17,395 for such equipment over a 10-year period.[3] By today's cost standards, his estimate is high. A more reasonable first-year estimate for a single-aisle system including one charge/discharge unit and protection for the entire book stock is $14,000. Annual outlays for the next nine years would be about $7500–$8000 for targets and $500 for maintenance.

Cost-benefit analysis does not reduce the difficulty of making the decision; it merely provides data upon which to base that decision. Calculating the ratio of benefits to costs is simple. The ratio is B/C. The resulting percentage represents the return on each invested dollar. Since benefits cannot be expected to outweigh costs in one year, a reasonable time span consistent with other library projects must be used. For instance, if an electronic security system costs $20,000, and $5000 worth of books are saved, the benefit-to-cost

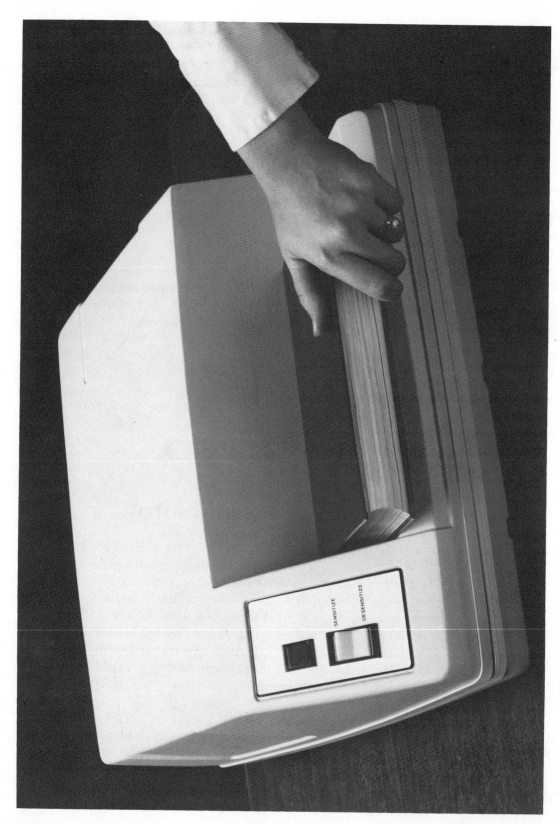

3M's 950 sensitizing/desensitizing unit accommodates oversized materials. *Courtesy 3M.*

ratio is $\dfrac{\$5000}{\$20,000}$ or .25. That means that for every dollar invested, only 25-cents' worth of benefits are accrued. In 20 years, however,

$$\frac{20 \times \$5000}{\$20,000 \text{ (first year's cost)} + 20 \times \$1000} = \frac{\$100,000}{40,000} = 2.5.$$

A dollar investment will yield $2.50 in benefits. In the above ratio $1000 represents the annual cost of the system (targets and service) after initial purchase and installation.

While the ratio is simple, deriving figures for benefits and costs is not. Before a library can calculate the benefits of an electronic security system, it must have a reliable estimate of annual losses attributable to theft. The experience of Washington University, described previously, indicates the difficulty of determining losses attributable to theft. After a three-year period, 60% of materials presumed stolen were returned to library shelves. Nor are returns the only consideration. Although some security systems are 100% effective, the effectiveness of most lies between 60% and 90%. In other words, an electronic security system will not prevent from disappearing all the materials that the library loses. There is also the possibility that a library would not choose to replace all the items that it lost. Although all the missing materials represent a cash loss, replacing half of them might be more cost-effective than purchasing an electronic security system.

In an article in the July 1974 issue of *College and Research Libraries*, Bommer and Ford suggest that subjective benefits to staff and patrons be included in a determination of B (benefits). The rationale is that confidence in the card catalog and speedy access to material have monetary value. According to Bommer and Ford, B should

- include processing costs for interlibrary loan requests for books missing from the library;

- take into consideration that electronic security systems are only 80%-90% effective; i.e., if $5000 worth of materials are missing, an electronic security system would only save $4000 worth.

Last, replacement costs must be determined. In a recent *Library Journal* article, Richard Boss set replacement costs at $30 per item.[4] While the figure is not too high, considering the *Publishers Weekly* estimate of current hardcover prices,[5] it will not be accurate for all libraries. For example, some school libraries have found that the typical replacement cost is between $11 and $13. Art libraries, on the other hand, would find $30 too low an estimate.

On the C (costs) side, costs for inserting targets should be determined, as well as those for equipment, installation, service and software (targets). Strips take more time to apply than labels—anywhere from 2 to 45 seconds. At the minimum, 20% of the collection should be targeted, as well as new acquisitions and any unprotected materials that are checked out. Often guard rails and architectural changes are necessary for proper installation and operation of electronic security systems. These represent additional expenses.

In April 1978 Griffith suggested that electronic security systems were economically sound investments for libraries losing between 450 and 500 books annually.[6] His projection is fairly sound. For example, a library that loses 500 books a year, 13% of which reappear at the end of the year, actually loses 435 books. If the electronic security system is assumed to be 80% effective, it will save 348 of those books. At a replacement cost of $15 each, this means a savings of $5220 a year, exclusive of subjective benefits. What a library will spend to secure those savings is approximately $5000 for sensing screens and control modules, $1300 for turnstiles or gates, $1300 for a charge/discharge unit, $500 for installation, $350 for service and $15,000 for software to protect 20% of 100,000 volumes. Excluding labor for target insertion, and additional installation fees, the total is $23,450. The library would pay for the system in about four years. If only half the lost volumes were replaced, the system would pay for itself in approximately eight years.

SUMMARY AND CONCLUSIONS

No electronic security system is 100% effective. In every one there is the possibility of target detection and removal. If this happens, of course, a book can be carried out through the sensing screens without triggering any alarm.

Various means of compromise and false alarms indicate that the technology of electronic article surveillance is far from perfect. It is, however, improving. In the past observers pointed out that if equipment was really reliable, large companies like 3M would emphasize retail applications, which represent an enormous potential market, rather than the fairly small library market. Over the last few years several have done just that. 3M actively entered the retail market in 1979; LPS has always been exclusively concerned with retail sales. Over 90% of Knogo's sales are to the retail market; in 1979 libraries accounted for only 37% of Checkpoint's sales.

The choice of which electronic security system to employ depends on a library's objectives and its budget. Briefly, if a library wants a bypass system now but envisions the need for converting to full-circulation later, Gaylord and Checkpoint are good choices because they make conversion simple.

If fear of radiation's effects is a primary concern, the Checkpoint and Sentronic (Book-Mark) systems have an advantage because they emit no radiation. Sentronic points out that while electromagnetic systems operate within the current U.S. standard for radiation frequency (10mW/cm square), this standard is 1000 times greater than that established by many European countries. Stop-Loss, for instance, was not marketable in Switzerland because its radiation level was too high.

If protecting audiovisual materials is important, a library might choose Knogo or Sentronic, which offer targets made especially for phonorecords. Knogo also has a charge/discharge unit specially designed to accommodate phonorecords and other flat materials. Other vendors have paid increasing attention to A/V material protection. For example, Checkpoint's Checklabel and its smaller Teeny Beeper label can be ordered with holes in the middle for easy application to phonorecords. Both Sentronic, and more recently, 3M have devised targets for cassettes.

If specific location of a concealed item is important, Sentronic (Book-Mark) and Checkpoint are likely choices. Both offer devices that indicate where an item is concealed and are usually used in retail operations. In addition, Stop-Loss, Knogo and 3M offer the least detectable strips; users indicate that Checkpoint has the fewest false alarms, the electromagnetic systems have a few and the magnetic systems have the most. In the past the Sentronic system was available with turnstiles only. Gates are currently being manufactured for that system. At present, therefore, all systems offer a choice of either entrance/exit gates or turnstiles. Turnstiles offer greater patron traffic control. Whereas only one person may exit through a turnstile at a time, several may exit simultaneously through entrance/exit gates—the exiting patron simply holds the gate open for persons behind him. Because some city and state fire codes prohibit the use of turnstiles, however, most vendors do not advertise their availability.

Cost is, of course, an important consideration. Table III-1 summarizes costs of the various electronic security systems. Since discounts are often available, the chart should be used as a rough gauge only.

Table III-1.   Cost Comparison for Electronic Security Systems

System	Sensing Screens (Single Aisle)	Charge/ Discharge Units (unit)	Entrance/ Exit Gates/ Turnstiles (unit)	Installation (Single Aisle)	Service (Annual)	Targets (unit)
Checkpoint Mark III	$4400	Not needed	$450 (manual) 500 (electric)	$250	7% of equipment purchase value	$.24
Gaylord/ Magnavox	5055	$ 675	520 (manual) 650 (electric)	750	$375	.13
Knogo IV	5000	1450	900	400	510	.10
Sentronic	5500	895*	595	500	400	.10
3M/1850	5475	1315	450–950	439	420	.15
3M/1350	4600	1315	450–950	439	270	.15

*Two units are needed.

One small but growing segment of the retail electronic security market is bookstores. Chapter IV discusses the need for bookstore security, its usefulness and the major differences between systems used in libraries and bookstores.

FOOTNOTES

1. Nancy H. Knight, "Theft Detection Systems Revisited: An Updated Survey," *Library Technology Reports,* May/June 1979, p. 334.

2. Knight, *Ibid.*, p. 230.

3. *Library Security Newsletter,* January 1975, p. 1.

4. Richard W. Boss, "The Library Security Myth," *Library Journal,* March 15, 1980, p. 683.

5. Chandler B. Grannis, "1979 Title Output and Average Prices: Preliminary Figures," *Publishers Weekly,* February 22, 1980, pp. 54-58.

6. J.W. Griffith, "Library Thefts: A Problem That Won't Go Away," *American Libraries,* April 1978, p. 226.

IV

Bookstores

Often as great as library loss, bookstore shrinkage (inventory loss) may be so serious as to threaten the survival of the retailer, especially the small independent one. In the bookstore trade, profit margins are traditionally low, sometimes only 3% of sales; therefore bookstore operators are particularly threatened by increases in theft.

Yet theft is on the rise. According to the U.S. Federal Bureau of Investigation's *Uniform Crime Report,* shoplifting increased 40% between 1973 and 1977.[1] *American Bookseller* reports inventory losses at almost 3% of nationwide sales.[2] According to a recent 3M investigation, professional fencing of books stolen in the U.S. is increasing.[3] Ronald E. Mason, chief of police at the University of Missouri at Columbia, estimates that campus bookstores lose between 5% and 6% of annual sales.[4] And individual reports of loss are numerous. Bill Fitzgerald, bookstore manager of the William Patterson College Bookstore (Wayne, NJ), noted steady increases in shrinkage; by 1977 it had reached 5% to 6% of gross sales. At the University of Utah Bookstore (Salt Lake City, UT), shrinkage was 6.6% in 1977. If only 2% of retail book sales, about $3 billion annually, were lost through theft, retailers would be losing $60 million, or $30 million at wholesale value.

Inflation adds to the problem. When *Publishers Weekly* polled 40 buyers and store managers representing more than 1150 nationwide book outlets in 1979, 29 retailers reported summer sales in excess of those for 1978; only 15, however, indicated that those gains were ahead of the then 13.4% current inflation rate.[5] Losses from theft, therefore, become even more painful to the retailer.

To deal with the problem of shrinkage, bookstores have used closed-circuit television, mirrors and parcel checks. Smaller stores have relied on observant cashiers; larger ones have hired guards. In the late 1970s, however, another option arose: electronic security. Individual stores began installing systems and the large chains began studying them. Anse Cates, Follett College Store Division's Midwest-North Regional Manager (Follett Publishing), feels that electronic security systems are not feasible for college stores, which handle large numbers of books in short periods of time. The inhibiting factor is staff time and cost. He thinks it unlikely that staff could find the time to insert targets in all the books that were to be protected. Librarians have estimated the cost of affixing such targets at $.05 for a strip and $.025 for a tag. Cates considers the time necessary to desensitize targets (turning them off so that they do not trigger alarms) before returning materials to publishers another time- and money-consuming procedure. Several stores, however, do not desensitize books before returning them.

TEST INSTALLATIONS

At Dalton and Walden bookstores, however, serious electronic security system studies are underway. Within the year, Dalton will have two test sites: a Knogo system in Atlanta and a 3M system in San Francisco. While interested in verifying both companies' claims that their systems can reduce shrinkage, Dalton hopes that the tests will do even more. It hopes to isolate the factors involved in theft. If an electronic security system reduces a 6% shrinkage to a 2% shrinkage, for example, one might assume two things: that the electronic security system is fairly effective or that 2% or perhaps 1% of the shrinkage is the result of internal theft. Tests should indicate whether theft is the result of external pilfering, internal pilfering or bad management (paper losses).

Tests should also help Dalton decide which items will be targeted—e.g., only volumes worth $15 or more, $25 or more, etc. In short, test results will both indicate the feasibility of electronic security and help to devise a strategy for its implementation. Even if systems are extremely successful, Dalton would probably install them only in stores suffering large losses.

For approximately two years Walden Books has had two New York test sites, one for LPS and one for 3M. While the second inventory has not been completed, the first one indicated that systems were effective. After second-year results are tallied, Walden will study the costs versus the benefits of security systems to determine which stores could afford to install them. While the determination about what items to target has not been made, Walden believes that the cost of targeting 100% of the stock would be prohibitive in 95% of cases.

COMPARISON OF BOOKSTORE AND LIBRARY FEATURES

Basically, all electronic security systems operate in the same way. All systems require that targets be inserted in items that are to be protected from theft. On a long-term basis, the targets may be the most expensive part of an electronic security system, depending on the number needed and the way in which they are used. In most retail applications, targets are reused, thus minimizing their cost. With books, however, a target can rarely be recycled. 3M targets are permanently affixed to books, concealed in the spine or between two pages. Sensormatic makes a SensorLabel, a peel-back covering that is placed over soft tags; at the point of sale, the precut portion of the SensorLabel can be torn off and the target can be used to protect another item. Unless attached to a wrapper, however, part of the SensorLabel remains on the book, which makes it difficult to return the item to the publisher. The same problem exists in the Checkpoint system when targets are affixed directly to books. Checkpoint has alleviated the problem somewhat by affixing a marker to a piece of cardboard that is inserted in a book and then removed when the book is sold. If a cardboard with a marker is removed from a book or a not-too-easily detected strip remains in it, there is no difficulty returning it to the publisher. In the latter circumstance, however, the target cannot be recycled.

Sensor screens are another standard component of an electronic security system. Targets affixed to merchandise are "active" or sensitized; they trigger audible or visual alarms when the merchandise is carried between two sensing columns, the pedestals or screens that detect the presence of an active target. To prevent the detecting apparatus in the columns from finding a target, the target is desensitized (made inactive). This is done in a variety of ways, depending on the system used. In libraries sensing screens are, for the most part, used in conjunction with either turnstiles or gates. When an active target is detected, the gate or turnstile automatically locks until a circulation attendant releases an alarm control. Anxious to encourage sales, however, bookstore operators forego turnstiles and gates. While this means a little less protection, it also means a savings of about $1000.

There is one overriding difference between the desensitizing needs of a library and a bookstore. Because books are continuously returned, a library needs the capacity to resensitize materials. In other words, it needs equipment that will make targets both active and inactive. Bookstores, on the other hand, need only to desensitize items at their point of sale. While it is true that booksellers may wish to make targets active again when items are returned, only the return of a substantial number of items would warrant the expense of an activator/deactivator (which usually costs about $1500). 3M provides a small, inexpensive brick-shaped deactivator especially for bookstore use. Capable of deactivating only, the 930 sells for about $100.

In addition to the absence of gates and reactivating equipment, there are some system-specific differences between the units marketed to libraries and those marketed to bookstores. The 930, 3M's small deactivator, is one such system-specific difference. Another is the varying frequency used by Checkpoint for its library and retail installations. All of Checkpoint's security systems operate on the principle of radio frequency; targets have tiny circuits, and sensing columns are receivers. To make sure that library books containing active targets do not trigger alarms when taken into retail stores (in bypass modes of operation, library electronic security systems use targets that are always active), Checkpoint operates systems on different frequencies. A bit like dialing different channels on a radio, the difference in frequency is usually 8.2 for libraries and 10.0 for retail stores (in Megahertz values).

Other vendors of library electronic security systems have made little provision for preventing active targets in library materials from triggering retail security system alarms. The problem is not an overwhelming one, however, since most other systems are rarely used in a bypass mode. In some instances an overlap is beneficial. At the University of Utah bookstore, for example, personnel often catch students who have borrowed library books without authorization, when students exit through the sensing screens of the bookstore's 3M Tattle-Tape system.

With the exceptions already outlined, systems sold to bookstores operate exactly like those sold to libraries (see Chapter III). Since bookstores, like libraries, have circulating collections, they purchase targets that can be sensitized and desensitized rather than permanently sensitized targets. When desensitizing targets by means of a shield rather than a sensitizing/desensitizing unit (as is necessary in the systems Sensormatic sold to libraries and the systems Checkpoint sells to libraries and retailers), libraries have traditionally used date due cards. Store operators shield targets in a different manner. Either they affix targets differently (Sensormatic's SensorLabel or Checkpoint's cardboard marker) or they cover targets with small "paid" or "thank you" stickers (Checkpoint's Teeny Beeper shields).

SYSTEMS AND COSTS

Five vendors of electronic security systems are currently marketing or attempting to market systems to bookstores. In order of the number of current bookstore installations, they are LPS, Sensormatic, Knogo, Checkpoint and 3M. Although LPS is currently being tested by Walden Books and has been fairly effective, it claims no other bookstore installations. Sensormatic, the leading vendor in the retail electronic security system market, has only three or four bookstore installations. Most are at New York City Barnes and Noble outlets, where they are used to protect expensive phono records only. The Knogo system, currently being tested by Dalton, has no U.S. bookstore installations but has approximately 15 overseas. Checkpoint has a number of overseas installations (many at gift stores), as well as about 18 U.S. independent and campus bookstore installations. Although 3M will not release a customer list, it was an early and active bookstore marketer. The company claims to have 100 bookstore installations, most of them in campus stores. A *Publishers Weekly* article notes installations at Naseralishah Bookshop (New York, NY), Words Worth Bookstore (Cambridge, MA) and University of Utah Bookstore (Salt Lake City, UT).[6] One additional location is the Yale Co-op (New Haven, CT).

With a few exceptions, the cost of bookstore systems is the same as that for libraries. Checkpoint charges $200 less for retail units because their electronics and circuitry are different. Software costs (targets) are also different. In a library system Teeny Beepers cost 18 cents each when bought in quantities of 5000. The unit cost for the same number of retail Teeny Beepers would be 12 cents. The scale reverses, however, when greater quantities are purchased. The unit cost of 50,000 Teeny Beepers would be 8 cents for libraries and 10 cents for retailers.

A Checkpoint library system with both an entrance and exit gate would cost approximately $5650; a retail system, only $4450. If the library acquired 10,000 books a year, Teeny Beepers would cost $1500 and CheckCards would cost a minimum of $300. For a retailer, costs would be $1280 ($1200 for Teeny Beepers and $80 for detuner "thank you" stickers). Labels affixed to book inserts, rather than the books themselves, could be reused. Bookstores purchasing 3M units have three models from which to choose, and prices range from $3600 to $5475 for single-corridor systems. The 1350, a middle-priced system, would cost libraries $8254; bookstores would pay $5139. Both Checkpoint and 3M prices include installation but exclude maintenance fees. Software costs would be the same for both, approximately $1150. Service represents an additional cost. Annual maintenance costs for the 3M 1350 would be $270; for Checkpoint it would be $411.50, 7% of the purchase price.

The complete price of an electronic security system for a bookstore targeting 10,000 volumes annually would be about $7000 for the first year and only about $1500 thereafter. Checkpoint costs approximately $7100; 3M's 1340 is approximately $6500 with a 930 deactivator and $7700 with a 950 activator/deactivator. If more than $7000 worth of sales are lost in a year or, to be more reasonable, more than $13,000 in sales are lost in five years, the bookstore can well afford an electronic security system.

The actual cost of each system may, of course, be lower than its list price. Additionally systems may be purchased under lease/purchase plans (see Chapter III), so that their costs can be amortized over several years. The owner of the Atlantic City News Agency, an independent Atlantic City, NJ, bookstore, figures that the monthly cost of the Checkpoint system, exclusive of software is $100. Tax credits and depreciation also make electronic security systems more affordable.

EFFECTIVENESS

The best information about the cost-effectiveness and operation of an electronic security system comes from bookstore operators themselves. At the Atlantic City News Agency, daily inventories indicated both the need for and the success of a Checkpoint Book Theft Detection System. The owner says that "unfortunately" the system does pay for itself—in other words, it has proven itself a cost-effective as well as a necessary evil. For the most part, only items costing $10 or more are protected. Some personnel indicate that the system is being compromised, something librarians have found true for years. Targets affixed to or inserted in items are removed. Sometimes "thank you" stickers are peeled off and used to shield other targets. For both librarians and booksellers, target detectability is of the utmost importance. While all institutions benefit from advertising that their premises are electronically protected, none benefit from patron knowledge of target location. Despite a few problems with compromise—*no* system claims to be 100% effective—Checkpoint is doing its job at the Atlantic City News Agency: it is reducing shrinkage.

At the William Patterson College Bookstore a Checkpoint system has been in operation for two years. Prior to its installation, shrinkage was between 5% and 6% of gross sales. After its installation, shrinkage was less than 3%. The system has reduced loss by more than 50% and has paid for itself. Bookstore manager Bill Fitzgerald estimates that any store with gross sales of $400,000 to $500,000 can afford an electronic security system. At those sales volumes, 6% shrinkage would cost between $24,000 and $30,000. If a system was only 50% effective, a $12,000 to $15,000 savings would be realized.

The Checkpoint system was chosen at William Patterson for two reasons. First, it was the least expensive system available. Also, the majority of thefts involved school supplies, equipment and clothing; therefore the difficulty of returning textbooks with visible markers in them to publishers—an inherent problem in the Checkpoint system—was unimportant.

In order to provide a measure of protection for textbooks, the textbook section was made a clerk-service area. Students could no longer browse for texts; they had to ask a clerk for the books they needed. Other sections of the store were targeted in one of two ways. Targets were inserted in clothing by means of a special pin or were affixed to objects or their wrappers (Checklabels come with adhesive on one side). Hard or semirigid clothing targets are detached with a special cordless magnetic detaching unit. Adhesive Checklabels or Teeny Beepers are deactivated when covered by a special sticker. Instead of attaching targets to items having a certain value, staff members target merchandise randomly. Special attention is paid to high-theft areas of the store.

While Checkpoint solves the problem of the particular kinds of losses sustained by the William Patterson College Bookstore, Mr. Fitzgerald indicates that the adhesive targets present a slight difficulty. They do not stick well on metal items like pen-and-pencil sets.

At the University of Utah Bookstore a 3M Tattle-Tape system with activating/deactivating units at each register has been in operation for three years. Prior to the system's installation in June of 1977, shrinkage had reached 6.6%. During the past fiscal year it was only 2.5%.

Theft trends at Utah were different from those at William Patterson. Instead of large losses in clothing and school supply sections, University of Utah Bookstore losses in those areas were not high enough to offset the labor costs for inserting targets. Book theft, on the other hand, was high. To reduce those losses 3M targets were affixed to all books costing $12.50 or more; other stock was targeted randomly. Since targets were concealed, there was no problem in returning books to publishers. They were sent back without being deactivated.

In addition to a Tattle-Tape system, the bookstore at Utah uses closed-circuit television for store surveillance and also employs guards at the beginning of each quarter to handle security-system alarms.

CHOOSING A SYSTEM

In the November 1979 issue of *American Bookseller*, Susan Gertman identified the two main issues confronting booksellers contemplating the use of an electronic security system: cost and customer reaction.[7] There are other factors that might determine a bookstore operator's choices. For example, all electronic security systems currently marketed to libraries and bookstores operate on low frequencies. As a result, sensing columns can be only about three or four feet apart. Higher-frequency systems—microwave systems, for example—permit much greater distances between sensing screens, but they are much more expensive. Bookstores with wide-open, mall-type entrances would probably not find currently available systems useful.

Further, the particular system chosen depends in large part on the kind of materials the bookseller needs to protect. Stores selling only books would probably prefer a system that allows books to be returned with no visible traces of electronic security targeting. Others should select a system with the software that is most compatible with their merchandise. 3M, for example, has developed a 6 1/2-inch by 1 1/8-inch by 3/16-inch reusable security target for clothing. Its regular strip, however, could not be affixed easily to a 4-inch by 3-inch jewelry case. Checkpoint and Sensormatic have targets for clothing and small items that are only a few inches long or wide; however, the adhesive target that can be used on books is visible and cannot be used on stock that might be returned to

3M Tattle-Tape system in use at the University of Utah Bookstore. *Courtesy 3M.*

publishers. Stores selling phono records will be especially interested in Checkpoint's and Sensormatic's 8-track tape and cassette display cases. Sensormatic has one case for tapes, the Keeper IV, and one case for cassettes, the Keeper III. Checkpoint's Checkpak accommodates both.

OUTLOOK

Relatively few bookstores presently employ electronic security systems. The company with the greatest number of bookstore installations has 2000 systems in libraries and only 100 in bookstores. Only one other vendor, Checkpoint, has U.S. bookstore installations in which books are actually protected. Yet competition is bound to increase and change the present marketing picture. Tests conducted by Walden and Dalton will have a major impact upon these changes, and may be responsible for introducing systems as yet untried by bookstore operators. Knogo and LPS are certainly interested in the bookstore market, and increased competition usually stimulates vendor response to customer needs. 3M's inexpensive deactivator, the 930, is just one indication of that trend.

FOOTNOTES

1. Joann Giusto, "3M's Tattle-Tape Squeals on Bookstore Shoplifters," *Publishers Weekly,* January 1, 1979, p. 34.
2. "The Wisdom of Security," *American Bookseller,* November 1979, p. 15.
3. Giusto, *op. cit.,* p. 35.
4. Beverly T. Watkins, "College Stores Lose Heavily to Thieves," *Chronicle of Higher Education,* May 5, 1980, p. 1.
5. "Retailers Begin to Feel Economic Pinch as Inflation Erodes Sales Gains," *Publishers Weekly,* August 20, 1979, p. 58.
6. Giusto, *op. cit.,* p. 35.
7. Susan Gertman, "Security Hardware," *American Bookseller,* November 1979, p. 16.

V

Library Users' Reports on Electronic Security Systems

In the spring and summer of 1980, 21 users of library electronic security systems were telephoned and asked the following questions:

- What size is the collection?
- How long has the security system been used?
- What materials are being protected?
- Are there false alarms and are targets easily detected?
- Has there been any increase in journal mutilation?
- How well has the system been accepted by staff and patrons?
- Have there been difficulties interfacing the system with an automated circulation system?
- Why was that particular security system purchased?
- Would the same system be purchased again?
- Have loss studies been conducted prior to or after installation of the security system?

This chapter reports users' responses to these questions. It also summarizes the results of earlier surveys, published in the November 1976 and May/June 1979 issues of *Library Technology Reports* (*LTR*) and the 1978-79 edition of *Book Theft and Library Security Systems*.

CHECKPOINT MARK II & MARK III

Fourteen out of the 25 libraries responding to the 1976 *LTR* survey indicated minimal false alarms with Checkpoint; only four reported any downtime (time when equipment was inoperative). While nine thought targets were detectable, only one library considered that a problem, and 12 out of 14 would have bought the system again. Three years later, 37 users agreed that false alarms (an average of 0.2 a day) and downtime were minimal; 29 would have bought the system again.

In the 1978-79 edition of *Book Theft and Library Security Systems,* Checkpoint users concurred on two things: there were almost no false alarms, and targets were easily identified. Only two considered detectability a problem.

Current Reports

The present survey confirms earlier reports. Reasons cited for purchase of Checkpoint were price, safety to patrons and safety to magnetic tapes. The system poses few mechanical problems, and three of the four libraries reporting would purchase it again.

Gulf Coast Community College
Learning Resource Center
5230 W. Highway 98
Panama City, FL 32401
Margaret Barefield, Head Librarian

This library, which houses 50,000 volumes, has used Checkpoint since August 1976 to protect records and video tapes as well as books. Safety was the primary selection criterion. The next-to-last inventory indicated a loss of 235 books; according to the latest inventory, only 73 books were unaccounted for. The library would purchase Checkpoint again.

East High School Library
515 N. 48th St.
Phoenix, AZ 85008
Lucille Crane, Department Chairman, Instructional Materials Center

Housing 25,000 volumes, the library has used Checkpoint to protect books since 1976. While several targets have been removed, their removal is not considered a problem. The system was purchased because of its price. It has presented no mechanical problems and would be selected again. One year prior to its installation, 1100 volumes were lost; one year later, only 300. System cost was amortized in one year.

Broadview Public Library
2226 S. 16th St.
Broadview, IL 60153
Marsha Erickson, Reference Librarian

Housing 45,000 books, the library has been using Checkpoint for 2½ years to protect films, phono records and books. Sometimes targets placed under bookpockets are removed, but the problem is minimal. Checkpoint was chosen because it does not damage magnetic tapes and because the absence of charge/discharge units makes the system less costly. Although no studies have been done to determine the system's effectiveness, it would be purchased again.

University of South Carolina
Thomas Cooper Library
1600 Sumter St.
Columbia, SC 29208
C.J. Cambre, Director of Libraries for Operations

The library, which contains about 1½ million volumes, has been using Checkpoint to protect calculators, typewriters, paintings and books for almost six years. The library was initially attracted to Checkpoint because of its reputation for minimal false alarms, and claims to have had only one in six years. Downtime is minimal. Despite all the pluses, the library is not sure that it would purchase Checkpoint again because of problems with targets. According to C.J. Cambre, on 25% of all targets the printed circuitry "bleeds through" the paper covering and makes black spots.

GAYLORD/MAGNAVOX

In 1976 Gaylord was new to electronic surveillance. The three respondents to the 1976 *LTR* survey made two basic comments: targets were easy to detect and false alarms were minimal. Three years later, reports were similar. All 26 respondents indicated minimal false alarms—a daily average of 1.2—and 15 thought targets easy to find. None considered this detectability a problem, and 23 of the 26 would purchase the same system again.

In the 1978-79 edition of *Book Theft and Library Security Systems,* users reported no significant problems with false alarms, but all thought targets easy to find. Two of the four would have purchased Gaylord again.

Current Reports

The most often cited reason for purchase of the Gaylord/Magnavox system is Gaylord's reputation. A few libraries reported mechanical, service and software difficulties; however, two out of four would definitely purchase Gaylord/Magnavox again.

Broward Community College
North Campus Library
1000 Coconut Creek Blvd.
Pompano Beach, FL 33060
Margaret Montondo, Librarian

Housing between 36,000 and 38,000 volumes, the library has had a Gaylord/Magnavox system in operation since the fall of 1979. Targets, used in books only, have been removed on occasion, and the library reports that one shipment of targets was defective. Adhesive on the back was weak; consequently several simply fell out after they had been affixed to books. Moreover, service has presented problems. It took some time to diagnose a malfunction in the system's control module because of the library's geographical location. Despite the difficulties, the system has reduced losses by 50%.

Addison Public Library
235 N. Kennedy Dr.
Addison, IL 60101
Patricia Kelly, Administrative Librarian

The library, which has 50,000 volumes, purchased the Gaylord/Magnavox system on the basis of Gaylord's reputation. It has been using the system for 10 months to protect both art prints and books. Only one target has ever been removed from library materials. Patricia Kelly believes placement is the key factor in detectability: targets put under bookpockets are not as visible as printed bookplate targets. Although there were some initial problems with a gate, there would be no hesitation about acquiring the same system again.

Allentown College of St. Francis de Sales Library
Center Valley, PA 18034
Brother James McCabe, Librarian

In use for two years, the Gaylord/Magnavox system protects the library's calculators, phono records and books, which number about 100,000. On a few occasions, especially when the system was first installed, targets were removed; neither that nor occasional false alarms triggered by watches or viewing screens are considered a problem. The system was selected because it gave the library a low bid and because other libraries in the area were using the same system and were satisfied with it. Prior to its installation approximately 700 books were lost in one year; after installation losses were less than 1% of that. According to Brother McCabe, the system "works well," and he would buy it again.

Washington Senior High School Library
7340 Leavenworth Rd.
Kansas City, KS 66109
Beth Harvey, Librarian

The library, which houses 18,000 to 19,000 books, has been using the Gaylord/Magnavox system to protect its book stock for 4½ years. For the first six months to a year, targets were removed. To counteract the difficulty, the library levied a $3 fine for target removal. There have been other problems with targets; some were not adhesive enough. Beth Harvey thinks the same system might be purchased again. Prior to installation the annual loss was 483 volumes; afterwards it was less than 100 volumes.

KNOGO MARK II & MARK IV

Six out of the 10 Knogo Mark II users responding to the 1976 *LTR* survey reported an average of six to seven false alarms a day. After some experience with the system, four users would have purchased it again. Three years later, when there were 30 respondents, the average daily number of false alarms was 2.4. Downtime was an average of 1.7 times a

Knogo has a variety of software targets for books and audiovisual collections. *Courtesy Knogo Corp.*

year, and all but one library indicated that service was available—as promised—within 48 hours. The general consensus: 97% (29 out of 30 respondents) would buy Knogo again.

Knogo system users reporting in the 1978-79 edition of *Book Theft and Library Security Systems* were attracted to the system because of low bid. Although two respondents thought false alarms were a problem, all four would have purchased Knogo again if its price remained the lowest available.

Current Reports

The most commonly expressed reason for purchasing Knogo was the availability of targets for audiovisual software. Two users reported false alarms, but all indicated that they would purchase the system again and that service was good.

Richmond Unified School District
1108 Bissell Ave.
Richmond, CA 94802
Roy Thayer, Director of Purchasing and Storage

Four Knogo systems have been installed in Richmond school districts. Two Mark IIs have been operating for two years, two Mark IVs for one year. Mark II systems were purchased because Knogo's downtime was minimal and site visits indicated that the system worked well. When additional systems were needed, Mark IVs were chosen on the basis of experience and for the sake of uniformity. Prior to the installation at Richmond High School, 500 books were lost in a year; after installation, only six books were unaccounted for. If prices remained comparable, the district would purchase the same system again.

Victor Valley Community College Library
18422 Bear Valley Rd.
Drawer 00
Victorville, CA 92392
Janet Bird, Head Librarian

A Knogo Mark IV has been protecting the library's 35,000 volumes, as well as its record and periodical collections, since January 1980. Selection criteria were the small size of the Knogo target and the availability of special targets for phono records. Although there are a few false alarms, triggered by briefcases and wheelchairs, and although one shipment of targets was unsensitized instead of sensitized, Janet Bird says that the library would purchase Knogo again. While it is too soon to conduct a full inventory, a weekly periodical survey indicates the system's effectiveness. In the past, 12 periodical issues would be missing in a week; now only one a week is unaccounted for.

Orange Glen High School Library
2200 Glenridge Rd.
Escondido, CA 92025
Jeannette George, Librarian

A Knogo Mark IV has been operating in this 15,000-volume library since January 1980. Although only books are protected, there are plans to protect phono records in the future. Availability of special audiovisual software is one reason the library chose Knogo. While target removal is a problem and it is still too soon to determine the system's effectiveness, the library would purchase Knogo again.

Beloit Public Library
409 Pleasant St.
Beloit, WI 53511
Alan Tollefson, Director

The Beloit Public Library purchased Knogo because it offered special audiovisual targets. A Mark II has been protecting record, periodical and book collections—the latter numbers about 80,000 volumes—for over a year. No study of the system's effectiveness has been conducted as yet, and there have been a few false alarms. However, service has been good and the library director is reasonably certain that the same system would be purchased again.

LPS INTERNATIONAL: STOP-LOSS

Stop-Loss was not being marketed in the United States in 1976, so it was not included in the *LTR* survey of that year. The system was first marketed in the United States in the summer of 1977, and although the company indicates that several systems have been installed in libraries, it would not provide a list of users. Therefore no users' comments could be elicited.

SENTRONIC (BOOK-MARK)

In 1976, 12 out of 21 users reported that there were false alarms; 10 out of 12 indicated that targets were easy to detect. In 1979 there were six respondents; only one of the six considered false alarms a major problem. Downtime varied from user to user. The general consensus: three out of the six would have purchased the same system again.

As reported in the 1978-79 edition of *Book Theft and Library Security Systems,* only one of four Sentronic users thought false alarms a major problem. Most thought targets too heavy, especially for use with unbound periodicals.

Current Reports

Two of the four Sentronic (Book-Mark) users contacted in the present survey had switched to different systems. Only one would consider purchasing Sentronic again. Causes for dissatisfaction were easy target removal, false alarms and poor service.

Alabama State University
Levi Watkins Learning Resource Center
Montgomery, AL 36109
John Buskey, Director

University of Alabama at Birmingham
Mervyn H. Sterne Library
University Station, AL 35294
Billy Pennington, Circulation Supervisor/Information Analyst

Both libraries had used Book-Mark systems. Alabama State switched to Checkpoint in 1978; the University of Alabama, to 3M in September 1979. The latter complained of easy target detection; the former, of false alarms and targets falling out.

Hammond Public Library
564 State St.
Hammond, IN 46320
Edward Hayward, Director

The library, which houses 70,000 volumes, purchased Sentronic in 1967 because Sentronic was the only system available at that time. No inventories had been conducted prior to the system's installation, which had been part of the contract for a new library building; as a result, the library has no way of determining the system's effectiveness. The director is dissatisfied with service. As an example, he reported that he was still awaiting delivery of a foot pedal ordered months earlier. There is some possibility that the same system would be purchased again, but all available systems would be reviewed before a selection was made.

Curry College
Louis R. Levin Memorial Library
1071 Blue Hill Ave.
Milton, MA 02186
Marshall Keyes, Director

Housing 85,000 volumes, the library purchased a Book-Mark system in 1973 to protect government documents and books. According to Marshall Keyes, some parts of the system are excellent. There has been no trouble with sensitizing/desensitizing equipment. On the other hand, targets are easily detected and removed, and, on the basis of service alone—it is handled by a local subcontractor—the system would not be purchased again.

City of Inglewood Public Library
101 W. Manchester Blvd.
Inglewood, CA 90301
Paul Klingen, Administrative Assistant

The main library, which contains 200,000 volumes, has used Book-Mark for three to four years to protect phono records and books. Originally purchased because of price, the same system would not be bought again. The library complains that targets are easy to detect and that they frequently fall out.

3M

Twenty out of the 27 Tattle-Tape users responding to the 1976 *LTR* survey reported some false alarms—three times a day for 12 users. Seventeen thought targets easy to detect, and 11 would have purchased the same system again. Three years later there were 59 respondents. False alarms occurred on an average of 2.2 times a day. Average downtime was 12.3 times a year. Fifty-six would have purchased the same system again.

In the 1978-79 edition of *Book Theft and Library Security Systems,* only one of four users identified false alarms as a major problem, and three would have purchased 3M again.

Current Reports

Although most users purchased 3M because its target was thought to be less visible than those used in other systems, three out of four users report some target removal. They also report little downtime and few false alarms. All four would buy 3M again.

S.R. Butler High School Library
3401 Holmes Ave.
Huntsville, AL 35805
Gloria Blood, Librarian

This 30,000-volume library has been using a Tattle-Tape system to protect books and magazines for three years. Although up to five strips weekly are removed from materials, the same system would be purchased again. Prior to its installation 500 books were lost annually; after its installation that number decreased to 100.

Sunnyvale Public Library
665 W. Olive Ave.
Sunnyvale, CA 94066
Ann Yingling, Technical Services Librarian

For two years a Tattle-Tape system has been protecting the library book collection, which numbers about 231,000 volumes. A low bid was the reason for its selection. While no studies have been made to determine the system's effectiveness, some attempted thefts have been detected, and Ann Yingling is reasonably certain that the same system would be purchased again.

Union College
MacKay Library-Learning Resource Center
1033 Springfield Ave.
Cranford, NJ 07016
John Holdorf, Associate Professor/Associate Librarian

For three years a Tattle-Tape system has been used to protect phono records, magazines and some of the library's 70,000 books. The system was chosen because its targets were thought less detectable than those used in other systems; however, some targets have been removed from library materials. The library would definitely purchase the same system again. The primary reason is because there is little downtime. In addition, losses in high-use areas, formerly 20% to 30%, have decreased to zero since the system's installation.

Belleville Area College Library
2500 Carlyle Rd.
Belleville, IL 62221
Bea Fries, Reference Librarian

The library, which houses 50,000 volumes, has been using Tattle-Tape for six years to protect magazines, pamphlets, cassettes, earphones and books. One reason for purchasing it was that its targets were less detectable than those of other systems. Only once or twice in six years have targets been removed. There has been some downtime; however, 3M has been very responsive to calls for service. The system paid for itself in two years. Prior to its installation, theft had increased steadily, creeping up from 300 to 600 to 800 books a year. Since Tattle-Tape's installation, no more than 150 books have been lost in any one year.

VI

Alternatives to Electronic Security Systems

Long before electronic surveillance equipment was available, libraries were combating the theft problem. Many employed exit guards, turnstiles, special patrols and closed stacks. They bought duplicates, gave moratoriums on fines and took legal action. These alternatives are still used, often along with electronic security systems; however, only rarely have studies been conducted to determine their effectiveness. Until such studies become available, programs can only be reviewed, not recommended. When evaluations were available they were included in the following review of alternative theft prevention programs.

GUARDS

Surveys in the late 1960s indicated that only about 50% of college libraries used any security system.[1] In the mid-1970s another study indicated that the percentage was closer to 33 1/3.[2] In both decades, however, many more libraries employed guarded turnstiles than electronic security systems. In the 1960s, when electronic systems were in the experimental stage, the consensus was that guarded mechanical turnstiles seemed to provide the best results. One study indicated that guarded turnstiles were employed by 80% of institutions using any security system.[3] In the 1970s Kneebone's poll of 97 academic libraries in Illinois indicated that one-third used guards and only one-fifth used electronic security systems; however, Kneebone found that electronic security systems were from 80% to 99.93% effective, while no statistical studies determined the effectiveness of guards.

The absence of studies makes any assessment of the guarded turnstile system difficult. Libraries usually assume that "checking is an excellent psychological deterrent" which eliminates "the removal of books in the library by sheer error."[4]

The assumption has some merit, since all theft prevention programs are more or less successful, but "more or less" is a shaky estimate on which to base a costly program. Matt Roberts of the Library of Congress points out several drawbacks of a guard system. Some libraries have more than one exit; hence several guards would be needed. Moreover, materials can leave the library through unauthorized exits, such as windows. Finally, thieves can foil guards by concealing stolen materials inside clothing. In addition, a 1967 survey showed that of the institutions using guards, only 14% reported checking purses.[5] Clearly, the guard or guarded turnstile system can never reduce theft by 100%—but neither can any system.

The decision to set up a theft prevention program is based on effectiveness and cost. One California school library found that one door guard reduced annual losses from 900 books to 239, which is about 73% effective.[6] If replacement costs are $20 per book, then the guard reduces that school's losses by approximately $13,000 a year. However, if the cost of the guard is $10,000 a year, the annual saving is only $3,000, and the benefit-cost ratio is relatively low.

The guard system is expensive, unless it is drastically modified, which is what one New York college has done. Door guards inspect the packages of exiting patrons for four weeks only—the two weeks before midterms and finals.[7] Obviously, such part-time guards will cost much less than full-time employees. And the cost of full-time guards must be measured against that for electronic systems, which involves a one-time investment followed by modest annual outlays for service and for sensitized pieces to be inserted in new books.

Beyond cost, however, is the deeper concern of how the public is best served. Some libraries may prefer the services of a friendly guard to electronic monitoring and staff surveillance; others will find the electronic systems less obtrusive and less threatening. Likewise, opinions differ on the use of special patrols, closed stacks, duplicate and amnesty programs, and legal action. Attitudes toward theft prevention are closely tied to the service concept: librarians feel that they serve the information needs of a community; they do not monitor behavior. No theft-prevention program in itself, however, destroys the service concept; the people administering the program are responsible for maintaining that concept.

PATROLS/BADGES

Some libraries have taken extreme measures to control losses; a recent survey of California high school libraries showed that 44% use unannounced locker checks to retrieve stolen and overdue books.[8] In some states such a search would be illegal; many other schools would shrink from such a policy.

Badges represent another security measure that has aroused controversy. They identify staff members engaged in routine library operations (such as serials binding) that might seem suspect if performed by unidentified persons. They also prevent nonstaff from entering restricted areas. In 1977 the Milwaukee Public Library instituted a policy requiring all library employees to wear identification badges.[9] Staff members carry photo identification cards in wallets and attach 2½-inch by 3-inch clip-on cards to their apparel. Earlier badges were larger and contained the following printed message: "May I help you?" Today the cards include the library's name and the designation "Staff." Such measures seem restrictive or are distasteful to some. Being tagged, watched and searched, after all, is not pleasant. But it serves a purpose, just as airport security checks help to prevent hijackings.

A security tactic of increasing interest is library patrolling. In small libraries and in those not plagued by many security problems, existing staff can often do the job. The trend, however, is to hire persons specifically for that task.

John Cogan, director of the Lehigh County Community Learning Resources Center in northeastern Pennsylvania, reports that his stacks are patrolled by staff members who tour the library at regular intervals to offer assistance to library users. It is a positive step, one which assures users that the library cares about them and about its materials.

At other institutions security personnel patrol the library. American University and Lehigh University employ a security guard. In 1980 the Bettendorf (IA) Public Library announced the employment of a "security person" to protect library property, decrease collection loss and reduce noise.[10] For two years Hofstra University Library (Hempstead, NY) has had two students patrolling the library's 10 open-stack areas for every hour that the library is open. Hired by the University's Security Department, the students wear bright yellow caps and windbreakers and carry walkie-talkies.

Unlike exit guards, patrol guards are not concerned exclusively with the unauthorized removal of library materials. Their concern is broader: the safety of staff, patrons, equipment, furniture and collections; they are also concerned about patron compliance with library use regulations. Therefore they often complement rather than substitute for book theft detection equipment.

LEGAL MEASURES

Most state laws provide a legal definition of library theft and a legal basis for dealing with thieves. In short, they recognize that taking, mutilating or failing to return library property is stealing. What most fail to do, however, is to define concealment of library property as theft and to protect library staff against suits for detaining suspected thieves. While more and more states are amending codes to include those provisions, it is impossible to calculate the effectiveness of laws and enforcement policies as theft deterrents. There is, on the other hand, abundant evidence that vigorous pursuit of overdue books enables the library to reclaim a quantity of material that might never have been returned to it otherwise.

In 1974 the Baltimore County Public Library (Towson, MD) hired a truant officer to collect overdue books and materials. In nine weeks $4000 worth of books and records from more than 100 borrowers was reclaimed.[11] In 1970 the Los Angeles Public Library System hired four field investigators to check on library materials that were more than six weeks overdue. In one year they brought back 7716 books valued at $42,706.[12]

At the Lawson McGhee Library (Knoxville, TN), John Ballard has been filling the post of delinquent book collector since 1976. Employed part-time, he reclaims overdue library materials for the entire county. Nineteen branch libraries forward overdue notices to the main library either monthly or bimonthly. After materials are outstanding for three or four months, Ballard goes to work, sometimes collecting two to three bags of material in a single day. The year prior to his employment, overdue materials cost the library between $12,000 and $15,000. After one year Ballard saved more than half that amount.

At the Lawson McGhee Library, fines are three cents a day, but they never exceed one dollar. At the Chicago Public Library a city ordinance passed in 1979 raised the overdue fine to a maximum of $500, a precedent already set at the Newark Public Library.[13] The NPL, which also employs truant officers or book detectives, actually posts a sign stating that unreturned books result in a $500 fine and/or 90 days in jail.[14] A Pennsylvania statute, which makes no provision for book theft, allows libraries to turn over to magistrates evidence of items that are four weeks overdue. And in Colorado a state law makes it a misdemeanor to willfully hold library books more than 30 days past due.[15] In 1979 a Penrose man went to jail for 90 days for failing to return overdue materials and for ignoring a 1977 court order that had directed him to pay $420 for the 130 books that he had outstanding.

Of course, all of these examples pertain to the recovery of books that have been properly checked out, and for which the library knows the identity of the borrower. The theft prevention measures discussed up to now, such as electronic security systems or guards, will not prevent patrons from checking out books in the normal fashion—and then keeping those books indefinitely. However, by combining measures to prevent unauthorized removal of books with steps to reclaim overdue books, libraries can cut overall losses.

Realizing how vital it is to enable libraries to do something about a suspected theft, as well as overdue books, Alex Ladenson, legal counsel to the Society of American Archivists' security program, has drafted a model law for library and archive theft. It identifies theft as willful concealment, exempts staff from criminal liability if they detain a patron for probable cause, and makes arrest without a warrant possible.[16]

Laws including those measures have been passed in Virginia in 1975, in Mississippi in 1978, in Iowa in 1979, and in Wisconsin in 1980. The Mississippi law, which is reprinted in Appendix I, makes theft or mutilation of library materials punishable by a fine of no more than $500 or by six months' imprisonment in the county jail, or both.[17] In addition to defining theft as willful concealment and permitting staff to legally detain patrons when there is probable cause, the Iowa law labels materials overdue six months as stolen.[18] The Virginia law has the following provisions:

> 42.1-72.   Injuring or destroying books and other property of libraries. — Any person who willfully, maliciously or wantonly writes upon, injures, defaces, tears, cuts, mutilates or destroys any book or other library property belonging to or in the custody of any public, county or regional library, the State library . . . [or any other library of an educational institution] shall be guilty of a class 1 misdemeanor.

> 42.1-73.   Concealment of book or other property while on premises of library; removal of book or other property from library. — Whoever, without authority, with the intention of converting to his own or another's use, willfully conceals a book or other library property, while still on the premises of such library, or willfully or without authority removes any book or other property . . . shall be deemed guilty of larceny thereof,

and upon conviction thereof shall be punished as provided by law.

42.1-73.1 Exemption from liability for arrest of suspected person. — A library or agent or employee of the library causing the arrest of any person pursuant to the provisions of 42.1-73, shall not be held civilly liable for unlawful detention, slander, malicious prosecution, false imprisonment, false arrest, or assault and battery of the person so arrested whether such arrest takes place on the premises of the library or after close pursuit from such premises by such agent or employee; provided that, in causing the arrest of such person, the library or agent or employee of the library had at the time of such arrest probable cause to believe that the person committed willful concealment of books or other library property.

42.1-74.1 "Book or other library property" defined. — The terms "book or other library property" as used in this chapter shall include any book, plate, picture, photograph, engraving, painting, drawing, map, newspaper, magazine, pamphlet, broadside, manuscript, document, letter, public record, microform, sound recording, audiovisual materials in any format, magnetic or other tapes, electronic data processing records, artifacts, or other documentary, written, or printed material, regardless of physical form or characteristics, belonging to, on loan to, or otherwise in the custody of any library, museum, repository of public or other records institution as specified in 42.1-72.[19]

Efforts to pass similar statutes are underway in Illinois, California and New York. In New York the current education law makes injury, defacement and destruction of library property punishable by fines or imprisonment or both—up to $500 or three years in a state prison or one in a county jail. Provisions under consideration at present are protection for private institutions, definition of library material, determination of worth of library material in terms of the market value for replacement, equation of concealment with theft, and ability to detain suspected offenders for a reasonable length of time.

As the present New York education law indicates, earlier statutes offer greater protection to public than to private libraries. There practices vary. At Hofstra University students are reported to the Dean of Students and outside borrowers are warned that they will be prosecuted if they return to the campus. At Princeton University offenders are put on two-year disciplinary probation. At the University of Wisconsin students caught stealing library materials are dismissed; their personal and academic records are destroyed. England's University of Warwick takes even stronger measures: offenders are turned over to the police to be prosecuted for larceny.[20]

The presence of a state statute does not mandate that libraries detain suspected thieves; it simply makes it legal to detain them if the library so chooses. Actually, only a few libraries do. While their number increases gradually each year, court costs and legal fees will probably deter many from taking action except in cases of major loss.

RESTRICTED ACCESS

Although closed stacks are standard in foreign academic and research libraries, they are unpopular in the United States, where a plethora of dissertations and articles defend browsing and direct access as key elements in research. Open shelves are the "American way." How much so is demonstrated by the response of undergraduates when they were denied access to the University of Toronto's new graduate research library in 1972; they rioted.[21] In the end, provisions were made for undergraduates to apply for access to the research facilities of the new library.

Unpopular as limited access is, most libraries protect their collections, to one degree or another, by closing stacks. Periodical collections in high school and college libraries are often closed, as are rare-book, manuscript and archival collections. Reserve systems and the tried-and-true "locked case," adjacent to the reference desk, which has preserved many a city directory and *Guinness Book of World Records,* are limited-access theft-prevention measures.

As thefts rise, more and more materials find their way behind closed doors. In spring of 1977 Princeton University finished an inventory of its collection and discovered that 37.5% of the books on functional analysis and nearly 14% of the most recent acquisitions were missing from the mathematics collection. To hold onto what remained and in light of a shrinking acquisitions budget, staff placed a number of materials previously in the open stacks behind locked glass breakfronts.[22] When materials began to disappear from the Brooklyn College (City University of New York) Library's heavily used vertical file, enterprising librarians bound popular items such as gun control information, assigned dummy call numbers to them and placed them behind the reference desk.[23]

Some would herald closed stacks as the perfect solution to a pressing and costly problem. In an article in *Law Library Journal,* Michael L. Richmond suggested that "the most effective method of keeping the patrons from direct access to the materials is to close the stacks."[24] Yet closed stacks are no more foolproof than are electronic security systems. Whereas the latter may be compromised in several ways, the former can and have been compromised by internal theft. In 1975, for example, the director of a Wilmington (DE) library directed library funds to his private art collection.[25] Other library directors have pilfered directly from collections. In late 1979 several valuable books were removed from the University of Buffalo Library by a janitor.[25]

Keeping stacks closed is not a perfect solution. It can also be expensive. Unless existing personnel can handle the new demands that restricted access creates, a staff increase is inevitable.

CIRCULATION SYSTEMS

In 1966 Robert and Haydee Clark proved that 22 different circulation systems and derivatives could be compromised. In fact, most circulation systems are so easily compromised that they are testimonials to the basic honesty of library users. All the premeditating thief need do is either destroy the book card and stamp the due date on the pocket or charge out one library book and return with the date due card to remove another book. The key word, however, is premeditated. The Clarks suggest that libraries sustaining significant losses should investigate whether their circulation system is responsible.[27]

REGISTRATION

In 1976 Canadian and U.S. libraries were warned that stolen IDs might be used to obtain library cards. Library cards were also stolen with the same object in mind—pilfering library books, records and equipment.[28] While libraries are defenseless against such premeditated thievery, they can minimize the misuse of library cards by requiring several pieces of identification for registration and limiting the number of books that circulate, until IDs are verified. In 1974, when the Baltimore County Public Library turned its overdue files over to a truant officer, it discovered that "one fifth of the delinquent accounts were found to have false addresses. . . ."[29] The Salt Lake County Library System (Salt Lake City, UT) requests double identification for library borrowing, and at least one ID must show a photograph.[30] At the Kearney (NJ) Public Library the first check-out is limited to one item.

In archival and manuscript collections, it is common practice to request and to hold a patron's driver's license while he uses restricted materials. If the license is stolen, however, the practice is ineffective. The Hobbs (NM) Public Library has a better idea. It requires a deposit in excess of the material's value. Until a $5 refundable deposit was charged for automobile repair manuals and high school equivalency handbooks, it was impossible for the library to keep copies of either on hand. There has been no such difficulty since 1977 when the policy went into effect. According to Jimmie Smith, assistant librarian, no one fails to return for the deposit.

Expanding this concept, several college and university libraries restrict library use to those with library cards. This forces students to validate their IDs, assures that outdated cards cannot be used to charge out material and certifies that current university records are available on each user. Such policies are not possible in all libraries. Among the reasons:

- Some college and university policies—or those of primary benefactors—provide that the library must serve the community as well as its own students and faculty.

- Some library administrators feel that such a step would violate their service concept.

- The growth of cooperative information networks that pool services and clientele would not be amenable to this restriction.

- Public library patrons do not always carry easily verifiable IDs.

DUPLICATES AND AMNESTY

In an effort to deter theft by accentuating the positive, many libraries, aware that greater use implies greater theft potential, buy duplicate copies of high-demand items. In

1968 Matt Roberts studied the connection between losses and available duplicate copies. No statistically significant correlation existed.[31] A 1972 Ohio State University Library study supports Roberts' conclusion. Of the books missing, 58% had duplicate copies and 9% had varying editions of the same title.[32] Only about 33% of the missing books were without other copies or editions. Rather than preventing or discouraging theft, duplicates provide a backup for items already stolen.

Another positive attempt to eliminate or minimize collection loss is an amnesty program. Libraries that encourage the return of books this way have been highly successful. The March 1975 issue of *Library Security Newsletter* reported that one Chicago school library offered a $30 raffle prize; the catch was that only students with cleared library records could participate. Ninety percent of overdues were returned. In 1975 the Greater Victoria Public Library sponsored an amnesty week. Returns were made at McDonald's hamburger outlets and free milkshakes were given for returning overdue items; over 12,000 were returned.[33] Using a similar approach, the Cumberland County Public Library (Fayetteville, NC) announced a moratorium on fines during National Library Week in 1979. To attract interest in the program, they offered a candlelight dinner at McDonald's to the person with the most creative excuse for an overdue.[34]

The idea of rewarding those who neglect to return library materials on time with free milkshakes and hamburgers is as noxious to some libraries as closed stacks are to others. Nevertheless, a well-publicized amnesty program works. In 1980, when the Geneva (NY) Free Library offered free french fries at Burger King to borrowers who brought materials back, long-overdue books returned to the library.[35]

BUILDING DESIGN

One of the most obvious elements of a security program can be the most overlooked: building design. The Cleveland State University Libraries discovered that building design was responsible for their extensive book loss. Several stairwells provided passage to unguarded elevators.[36] The C.W. Post Center of Long Island University discovered a loss rate of more than 10% shortly after moving into a new facility in which control of exits was difficult.[37] After Union College Library (Cranford, NJ) installed a 3M system, its losses, formerly 20 to 30% in some subject areas, dropped to zero. Losses have been creeping slowly upward since the first year, however, because a windowed second-floor lobby extends beyond the sensing units positioned on the first floor.

After Chicago's Newberry Library lost 11 valuable maps, an architect was asked to draw up plans for a complete redesign of the first floor.[38] Langmead and Beckman's guidelines for the construction of academic library buildings state: "Whether the stacks are open or closed, it should be possible to design the library so that there is one controlled exit through which all library users must pass before reaching the exterior doors."[39]

One of the first steps taken by representatives from electronic security system companies is to analyze entrance/exit patterns; professionals in the security field realize that good traffic control is the basis for circulation control. Langmead, an architect, and Beckman, a systems librarian, write unflinchingly that "the concept of checking each book as it leaves the college library to determine if it is correctly charged out is a necessary concomitant to an efficient operation." Exit control makes the book check possible.

No such statements are usually made about nonacademic libraries. Standards exist regulating building space, collection size and staff size, but few exist concerning security. Whether building a new library or re-evaluating an old one, a conscious effort should be made to reduce traffic to one main entrance and exit (fire doors excluded).

In offering advice on building a new library, John W. Powell, past director of security at Yale University, recommends that "security be discussed and included in any negotiations with architectural firms."[40] Libraries can insist that the architectural firm hire special security consultants. Careful preplanning saves money. A great deal of effort went into the construction of the Beinecke Rare Book and Manuscript Library at Yale University. Sophisticated systems controlling humidity, temperature and possible fires were installed. One night, however, a student foiled the magnetic door alarm system and gained access to the collection with a coat hanger. According to Powell, the intrusion system installed thereafter "cost at least ten times what it would have if planned during construction. . . ." All libraries will not need extensive protection beyond exit controls. However, the library's total security needs should be determined—prior to construction—by the librarian, who knows the community's behavior and preferences, and the security consultant, who knows what protection systems are available.

SECURITY CONSCIOUSNESS

In 1978 Sergeant Alex Shearer told Scottish librarians that the first and most important theft-prevention step was staff education.[41] At present two kits are available for that purpose. The first, produced by the Library Council of Metropolitan Milwaukee (LCOMM) includes a 16mm film or 3/4-inch video tape, discussion guide, workshop outline, bibliography and sample security policies. A 113-page Association of Research Libraries (ARL) report, "Theft Detection and Prevention in Academic Libraries" (SPEC Flyer and Kit #37), includes discussions about purchasing electronic security systems and ARL members' solutions to theft and mutilation. The LCOMM kit costs $15 to rent and $140 (film) or $50 (video tape) to purchase. ARL material costs $7.50 for members and $15 for others (both prepaid).

Educating staff, however, involves more than showing films and circulating articles and reports. It means stressing what is obviously true: that "no precaution, safeguard or deterrent will be successful without the constant alertness and supervision of the library staff."[42] The heart of the matter is that, with the exception of duplicates, any collection security tactic *can be* successful. An amnesty program can secure as many returns as a truant officer. Programs do not fail because they are negative or succeed because they are positive. Hence the endless debate that the other person's system is morally wrong and therefore ineffective is absurd. What is important is that the library believe that something should be done—and that something must satisfy the heart and budget of the library and the community. If the staff sincerely believes that theft is a problem and is committed to combating it in some systematic fashion, then the library is already on the way to winning the battle for an effective security program.

FOOTNOTES

1. "60-College Security Study Finds Few Satisfied," *Library Journal,* May 7, 1968, p. 1848.

2. Ted Kneebone, "Library Materials That Go AWOL or the Issue of Security in Illinois Academic Libraries," *Illinois Libraries,* May 1975, p. 341.

3. Ernest E. Weyhrauch and Mary Thurman, "Turnstiles, Checkers, and Library Security," *Southeastern Libraries*, Summer 1968, p. 112.

4. Weyhrauch, *ibid., p.* 114.

5. *Ibid.,* p. 112.

6. *Library Security Newsletter,* January 1975, p. 12.

7. *Library Security Newsletter,* March 1975, p. 10.

8. *Library Security Newsletter,* January 1975, p. 12.

9. "Security Badges in Milwaukee," *Library Journal,* June 1, 1977, p. 1230.

10. "Security Person at Bettendorf," *Library Journal,* February 1, 1980, p. 345.

11. "Truancy Procedures at Baltimore County Public Library," *Library Security Newsletter,* January 1975, p. 11.

12. "LAPL Lowers the Boom on Book Thefts," *Library Journal,* January 1, 1970, p. 20.

13. "$500 Fines at CPL," *Library Journal,* August 1979, p. 1510.

14. "Overdues and Book Truancy," *Library Security Newsletter,* May/June 1975, p. 12.

15. "Don't Mess With This Library," *Morning Call,* February 4, 1979, p. A-8.

16. "A Model Law Relating to Library and Archives Theft, *Archival Security Newsletter,* March 1977, p. 7.

17. "Bedeviled Libraries—Is It Bibliomania?" *Mississippi Library News,* June 1978, p. 75.

18. "Iowa Throws the Book at Thieves, Delinquent Patrons," *Library Journal,* August 1979, p. 1510.

19. Edmund Berkeley, Jr., "Code of Virginia Revised to Benefit Libraries and Archivists," *Virginia Librarian,* May 1975, p. A.

20. "Princeton Cuts Acquisitions: Theft on the Upswing," *Library Journal,* May 1, 1978, p. 918.

21. "University of Toronto Settles Access Issue," *Library Journal,* June 15, 1972, p. 2140.

22. "Bedeviled Libraries," *op cit.,* p. 92.

23. Andrew Garoogian, "Making Book at the Reference Desk," *Library Journal,* June 15, 1978, p. 1235.

24. Michael L. Richmond, "Attitudes of Law Librarians to Theft and Mutilation Control Methods," *Law Library Journal,* February 1, 1975, pp. 60-70.

25. "Wilmington Director Faces Trial For Theft," *Library Journal,* August 1975, p. 1366.

26. "UB Library Losses To Be Detailed Soon," *Buffalo Evening News,* October 3, 1979, p. 39.

27. Robert F. and Haydee Clark, "Your Charging System: Is It Thiefproof?" *Library Journal,* February 1, 1966, p. 642.

28. "Theft Via Stolen Identification," *Library Journal,* March 15, 1976, p. 768.

29. "Truancy Procedures at Baltimore County Public Library," *Library Security Newsletter,* January 1975, p. 11.

30. "Double Identification for Library Borrowing Urged," *Library Security Newsletter,* Spring 1976, p. 22.

31. Matt Roberts, "Guards, Turnstiles, Electronic Devices, and the Illusion of Security," *College and Research Libraries,* July 1968, pp. 269, 270.

32. Allyne Beach and Kaye Gapen, "Library Book Theft: A Case Study," *College and Research Libraries,* March 1977, pp. 118-28.

33. "Amnesty Week Reaps 12,000 Overdue Books," *Feliciter,* June 1975, p. 8.

34. "No Fines and Tall Tales," *Library Journal,* June 1, 1979, p. 1207.

35. "Burgers for Overdues," *Library Journal,* March 15, 1980, p. 669.

36. "Cleveland Book Heist: Building Design Blamed," *Library Journal,* June 15, 1975, p. 1173.

37. Donald L. Ungarelli, "Excerpts—Taken From a Paper Entitled *The Empty Shelves,*" *The Bookmark,* May-June 1973, p. 155.

38. "Yale and Newberry Recover Stolen Maps," *American Libraries,* March 1979, p. 100.

39. Stephen Langmead and Margaret Beckman, *New Library Design: Guide Lines to Planning Academic Library Buildings,* (New York: John Wiley & Sons, 1970), p. 28.

40. John W. Powell, "Architects, Security Consultants and Security Planning for New Libraries," *Library Security Newsletter,* September-October 1975, p. 6.

41. Sergeant Alex Shearer, "Essentials of Library Security—The Police View," *SLA News,* 1978, p. 45.

42. Norma E.S. Armstrong, "Essentials of Library Security—The Librarian's View," *SLA News,* 1978, p. 57.

VII

Journal, Nonprint and Special Collection Protection

JOURNALS

Estimates of journal loss should be readily available, since the binding process constitutes an ongoing inventory of current issues. Nevertheless, such information is rarely published. A 1969 inventory of the Johns Hopkins University Library showed that 301 of 3257 serial volumes in LC classification categories A-E were lost.[1] Beyond this, documentation is sparse.

Mutilation of Journals

Reports of journal mutilation are not so sparse. A 1972 survey of college and university libraries indicated that periodical mutilation was a serious problem for 80% of them.[2] According to a 1976 *Library Security Newsletter* article, mutilation "plagues most public libraries, as well as school libraries. . . ."[3] In 1978 Stanford University's Lane Medical Library reported increased journal mutilation.[4]

In some ways technology is responsible for increased journal mutilation. The need for up-to-date information in an age of rapid technological change has made the journal a primary research tool. Online bibliographic retrieval, which makes long lists of journal references available in a relatively short time, increases the demand for periodical information.

Articles ripped out from journals and well-concealed by a thief will not be detected by guards or security systems. Often the presence of either one encourages some users, who might have borrowed periodical volumes and returned them later, to tear out an article and keep it. *Library Journal* (June 15, 1975) reported that after the University of North Carolina installed the Tattle-Tape electronic security system, theft rates decreased but mutilation rates increased. There were similar results at Upsala College (East Orange, NJ) after an electronic security system was installed.[5] Half of the U.S. libraries responding to a recent questionnaire indicated that while book theft dropped after installation of an electronic security system, journal mutilation increased.[6]

The presence, quantity and quality of photoduplication equipment also affects journal mutilation. Although the East High School Library (Phoenix, AZ) has had a Checkpoint theft detection system in operation for four or five years, mutilation is a persistent problem. The reason: there is no money in the budget for a photocopying machine. Photoduplication can also be costly and time-consuming, and some machines will not reproduce fine print, tables, charts and color illustrations.

As though the periodical collection were not beset by enough problems, it also is the target of the professional thief. In 1971 an individual representing himself as an official of Microforms, Inc., negotiated a two-month loan of 11 periodical sets for microfilming from Ohio Northern University (Ada, OH). His credentials were checked at the Chamber of Commerce and the Better Business Bureau; however, after two months neither he nor the periodicals could be found. Several months later four sets were discovered to have been sold to the J.S. Canner Co. in Boston.[7]

In the same year the California Academy of Sciences Library (San Francisco) discovered many valuable volumes of *Curtis's Botanical Magazine* missing. It publicized the loss, and shortly thereafter the University of California at Davis discovered that its set of the first 42 volumes of *Curtis's Botanical Magazine* was also gone.[8] In 1976 northeastern libraries from Maine to Pennsylvania discovered pages missing from 19th-century journals: all were plates by Winslow Homer. A full set of the artist's engravings for *Harper's Weekly* are valued at $6000.[9]

Because periodical material is in great demand, is increasingly expensive and is susceptible to mutilation in a way that books usually are not, journal theft and damage represent a particularly acute problem. Exit guards, turnstiles and/or sensing screens, all of which function as psychological deterrents to book theft, are ineffectual deterrents to journal mutilation.

Protective Measures

It is unsurprising, then, that few answers to the problem exist. There are the obvious remedies: obtaining subscriptions on microfilm is one. After one small medical library converted 118 of its 160 journal titles to microform, it discovered that no volumes were stolen or defaced.[10] Another solution might be the purchase of more, better and less expensive photocopy machines (although the new copyright law, which took effect in 1978, puts certain restrictions on photocopying). At some libraries—Stanford's Lane Medical Library and the Murrey Atkins Library at the University of North Carolina at Charlotte—inexpensive photocopying equipment has not minimized mutilation; at others it has.

There are less obvious remedies. In January 1970 *Library Journal* reported that the Arlington Heights Memorial Library in Illinois had installed a "controversial video monitoring system." Used for four years to deter collection theft and for surveillance of problem areas where groups might congregate, the system was eventually replaced with the

Checkpoint electronic security system for three reasons. There were some difficulties repairing equipment, staff often neglected to pay attention to the video monitor and cameras were stationary, offering limited views, thus cutting back on effectiveness. Video monitors are still used by libraries, but for other security programs, such as surveillance of the parking lot.

There are novel remedies. The library at Georgia Institute of Technology paints colored stripes (one green, one purple and one orange) on the edges and spines of unbound periodicals, serials, government documents and technical reports so that these materials can be seen easily, especially by door checkers examining briefcases and book bags.

There is no single solution to the problem of mutilation in all libraries. The best remedies go to the heart of the matter—the interaction between library services and patrons' needs. At the East Islip (NY) Public Library, for example, staff maintain a give-away picture file for youngsters. Pictures are taken from old encyclopedias and periodical issues. By allowing each child to take two free pictures, the library has reduced mutilation of its juvenile collection.[11] At the Moody Medical Library (University of Texas Medical Branch, Galveston), the tactic is somewhat different: *Playboy* centerfolds are removed before issues go on the shelves.[12] In both cases solutions resulted from an analysis of the kind of mutilation that the library collection sustained.

Closing stacks is another way to make sure that patrons can find the articles they need. Closed stacks also offer the library more control over its periodical collection. They make it possible to collect statistics on usage to help make decisions about acquisitions, to reduce interlibrary loans for articles that should be available in the library but are missing, to inspect journals for mutilation when they are returned and to gather issues to be discarded or bound.

An equally promising solution may be based on a study by Eugene Garfield, who searched for 161 journal articles cited more than 75 times between 1961 and 1973. He found that "an unacceptably large number of articles had been ripped from the journals," and suggested that libraries "prepare bound volumes of highly cited journal articles separately from the rest of their collection. . . ."[13] There is the germ of an excellent idea in the suggestion, which unites patron needs and library service. The Brooklyn College library, which binds vertical file material and keeps it behind the reference desk, has already followed it up. While it would be inconvenient for libraries to house heavily demanded journal volumes separately, articles cited 75 times or more could be photocopied and made available at the circulation desk for overnight circulation. The original article could be stamped: "Additional copies of this article are available for overnight charging at the circulation desk." Under the new copyright law, some payment of royalties might be required, depending on how many copies are made.

Whatever approach is used—closed stacks, color coding, electronic devices, staff surveillance or video monitoring—an effort should be made to let the public know how costly and difficult it is to replace periodicals. One Kent State University student who admitted to journal mutilation said, "It definitely would have made a difference to me if I'd known they couldn't replace the articles."[14] It would make a difference to most library users.

NONPRINT MATERIALS

In 1977 Herbert Katzenstein reported the following losses of audiovisual and office equipment:[15]

- In the Bronx, NY, the staff of a newly designed learning resource center eagerly awaited the arrival of hardware and software for a reading program. Shortly after the materials arrived, the building keys were stolen and most of the equipment was taken.

- Over the summer months the video tape and instructional technology equipment of a New Jersey suburban school disappeared.

- One New York City public school was forced to send its reports to another school to be typed; during the night its own adding machine and typewriters had been stolen.[16]

The resale value of office equipment and audiovisual hardware makes them the target of the professional thief. But this is not the only nonprint material attractive to the professional. As more libraries assume the role of community cultural centers, the incidence of art theft increases. In 1976 the Malden (MA) Public Library reported the loss of an 1873 Winslow Homer oil painting, *Whittling Boy*; it was valued at $100,000. The same year the Portland (ME) Public Library discovered that 13 oil paintings, a bronze statuette, a grandfather clock and four Chinese vases had been taken from the archives.[16] In 1977 the Harwood Foundation Library in Taos, NM, lost three paintings valued at $15,000. The same year, one year prior to the installation of a Knogo book theft detection system, the Highland Park (IL) Public Library lost 33% of its popular music records.[17] In the first six months of 1979 the Chicago Public Library lost $7000 in films.[18] During the same year the Wilmot branch of the Tucson (AZ) Public Library reported that 52%, or 3590 nonprint materials were missing. The figure was slightly higher at the Woods branch: 54% of all nonprint materials and 64% of phono records.[19]

Not all libraries suffer serious losses of nonprint materials. For instance, the Instructional Materials Center of Eisenhower High School in New Berlin, WI, which uses integrated shelving of media, calculated the following losses after taking inventory in 1974-1975: 15 out of 1404 filmstrips; 102 out of 1017 cassette tapes; one LP record; 23 out of 6923 slides. Over six or seven years, only one television receiver, calculator, wall clock and 20-inch fan disappeared from the University of Wisconsin's Pierce Library.[20] Similarly low losses were reported by the Lehigh County Community College Library in Pennsylvania, which shelves media openly but separately. Only two audio tapes (out of 215) and two filmstrips with records (out of 384) were lost as of the 1977 inventory. Book losses, however, were substantially higher: 614 in 1977. In both media centers the "book, pamphlet and magazine losses far exceed the number of lost and damaged nonprint materials."[21]

What are the implications of this relatively low loss figure? It is possible that audiovisual materials are not used as frequently as books, and therefore fewer are stolen. They also represent a small portion of the collection for most libraries. Still, hardware is in greater need of protection than software, art works excepted. The substantial losses reported by Katzenstein were hardware losses.

Protecting Audiovisual Hardware

Librarians and media specialists in New York City found that the following guidelines protected audiovisual hardware:[22]

- Using permanent paint to mark two sides and all removable parts with serial numbers makes equipment less attractive for resale.

- Engraving identification numbers on metal parts with an electric etcher makes a relatively permanent mark. (One school district suggests that serial numbers be engraved on two different areas of the equipment, since a thief is likely to remove only the first engraving.[23])

- Storing equipment in unmarked closets or rooms may protect it from thieves unfamiliar with library operations.

- Using steel doors with solid hinges and bolt locks, provided vents for temperature control are included, frustrates burglaries.

- Warning posters or stamps placed on equipment alert the thief that it is traceable if stolen.

- Advertising losses in the community sometimes leads to the items' return.

- Installing convex detection mirrors reduces the chance of equipment loss.

There are, additionally, a number of security devices available to protect hardware. *Library Security Newsletter* has reported the following to be useful:

- marker pens that write invisibly on surfaces but engrave serial numbers that are visible under ultraviolet light;

- cables that secure calculators, adding machines, projectors and photographs;

- diamond-needle locks;

- removable cartridges;

- bolts to secure typewriters and turntables.

The best protection against unpremeditated thefts, however, is adequate control over equipment records, storage and circulation. The value of and necessity for accurate records of equipment owned is obvious, and it is not the purpose of this chapter to outline procedures for inventory and service-record control of such equipment. But setting up such procedures is not difficult. Frank A. Jerome outlines a simple KARDEX record keeping form in the March 1975 issue of *Audiovisual Instruction*.

At Lehigh County Community College, the library administers the school's A/V programs. In the campus A/V center, film, slide, overhead and opaque projectors, record players, tape recorders and all other equipment are arranged in neat rows. Each row contains four pieces of equipment. A large board by the front door duplicates the arrangement of equipment. If an item is in use, the request form is placed on the board map where the equipment was located. This is an excellent ongoing equipment check. If an item is not in a row and no slip on the board indicates it is in use, an immediate check can be made.

Here are some other tips: be sure that if some audiovisual equipment is out in the open, its use is supervised; have students borrowing head sets leave their IDs at the desk until the head sets are returned; restrict circulation of A/V equipment. Many libraries circulate only cassette players to students/patrons. Other equipment is restricted to use by faculty and administration.

Protecting Audiovisual Software

Audiovisual materials are usually housed separately from other materials in the library, and although stacks are not closed, materials do not circulate. While this should afford maximum protection, most materials can also be protected by electronic security systems.

High-theft items are audio tapes and records. To protect them, some libraries dub the sound onto cassette tapes, keeping the masters in the noncirculating collection and circulating only the cassette tapes. (This practice may be limited by the new copyright law.)

An expansion of the same idea has made nonprint theft and mutilation virtually nonexistent at New York University's library for the graduate faculty of art history and archaeology, the Institute of Fine Arts. So that slides shown in classes may be taken home for review, they are photographed and the resulting negatives are copied. Student illustrations can be reproduced with photographic equipment located in the mezzanine. Even rare books have been made more accessible through photoduplication. In one instance, a rare out-of-print volume was microfilmed; in another, when drawings in a rare volume would not reproduce well in microform, they were photographed. The text was microfilmed, then blown back on reader printers for additional copies.[24]

It is good practice to inventory audiovisual materials yearly. By doing so, the library can form policies to deal with special theft problems. For instance, in 1971-72 the Eisenhower High School Library in New Berlin (WI) discovered during inventory that 175 out of 397 cassette tapes were missing. The school re-evaluated its policy for checking out blank cassette tapes for class projects and decided to simplify the check-out procedure. As a result, only 97 out of 624 tapes were missing the following year. In 1973-74 losses were reduced to 79 out of 805 tapes.

Certain nonprint materials such as valuable art works require special attention. A detection tag gives little protection: it is not likely that professional thieves will walk past sensing screens. When the Malden Public Library's Winslow Homer oil painting was stolen, the thieves vaulted a four-foot gate; the theft occurred during regular library hours, foiling a burglar alarm system that worked only on weekends and at nights.

The American Association for State and Local History provides information on ways to protect art exhibits. Technical Leaflet #99 may be ordered from the Society at 1400 8th Avenue S., Nashville, TN 32703.

SPECIAL COLLECTIONS: RARE BOOKS, MANUSCRIPTS AND ARCHIVES

In 1975 Philip Mason, director of the Archives of Labor and Urban Affairs at Wayne State University, wrote, "Theft from archives has now reached alarming proportions." He cited evidence that the trend will continue, noting: "The major reason for theft from archives has been monetary gain."[25] Several examples illustrate the problem:

- In 1972 three rare books valued together at $10,000 were stolen from the British Museum Library. Thereafter, stricter proofs of identity were required, and bags and briefcases were inspected before patrons were allowed to leave.[26]

- In 1973 the New Mexico State University Library lost 4000 historical documents. The thief, Arvil Howard Elam, "gained access to the closed stacks . . . by claiming to be the grandson of New Mexico pioneer merchant Charles Ilfeld."[27]

- In 1974 Carolyn Sung reported the loss of the Felix Frankfurter diaries and papers from the manuscript division of the Library of Congress. That and other thefts have led to a complete revamping of the institution's security regulations.[28]

- In 1977 the Carnegie Library of Pittsburgh reported the loss of 11 music scores. Ten were rare and valuable.[29]

- In 1979 a Tulane University professor was convicted and served a one-year prison term for removing five valuable maps from Yale's Sterling Library and several others from Chicago's Newberry Library.[30]

Cooperative Efforts

Because archival materials are sold by and to a limited audience, because they are often irreplaceable and easily identifiable, and because they are costly and therefore the target of the professional thief, archivists have made organized efforts to curb losses. One early cooperative effort took place in London in 1972. The Rare Books Group of the British Library Association met with the Antiquarian Booksellers' Association to discuss book theft.[31] Rejecting such mechanical aids as closed-circuit television, electronic security systems and expensive alarm systems, the groups placed greater emphasis on controlling access, identifying materials as library property, and admitting and reporting losses.

The last issue was of paramount importance. As late as 1975 John M. Kinney, director of the State Archives at Texas State Library, was convinced that "the biggest archival security problem is that of convincing archivists and their staffs that there *is* a problem!" Kinney suggested that "most institutions do not publicize their losses," and that "sometimes the institution itself does not know that a theft has occurred."[32]

The Antiquarian Booksellers' Association and Rare Books Group faced the problem head-on and came up with two ways of dealing with losses: a joint insurance scheme to which libraries and booksellers would contribute, and the preparation of a national register of stolen items. The second idea became a main part of the Society of American Archivists' security program, developed in 1975 and funded by the National Endowment for the Humanities.

Society of American Archivists

The Society of American Archivists (SAA), which represents archivists in the United States, Canada and other countries in the western hemisphere, publishes the *National Register of Lost or Stolen Archival Materials.* The list is updated bimonthly and distributed to hundreds of manuscript dealers and curators across the country. Primarily a list of manuscript materials, printed materials are included if they can be identified by unique or distinguishable markings. Other items such as photographs, films, books, microfilms, artifacts and maps can be registered if they are one of a kind.[33] All listed items must have been lost or missing for less than 20 years; little chance exists for recovering materials missing longer than that. No charge is made to report missing items; one need not be an SAA member. Registration forms for missing items are available from SAA Archival Security Program, Box 8198, University of Illinois, Chicago Circle, Chicago, IL 60680.

The *National Register* can also act as a clearinghouse for information on archival theft. Details of *modus operandi,* descriptions of suspected thieves, and names of dealers and collectors known to buy stolen materials can be indexed, creating a network of valuable data for both libraries and law enforcement personnel.

In addition to the *National Register,* the SAA has published a manual on archival security: Timothy Walch's *Archives and Manuscripts: Security,* available at a cost of $4 to members and $5 to others. *Archival Security Newsletter,* an SAA publication, reports thefts, recoveries and security reminders and developments.

Since February 1, 1977, the Society has also been offering a consultant service. The program provides libraries with the specialized professional help needed to plan and implement a security program. Consultants are kept up-to-date on procedures for marking manuscripts, library security and the law, and on electronic security devices. The service is run on a cost-sharing basis; the Society pays the consultant's professional fees and the institution absorbs travel, room and board expenses for the consultant's two-day visit. The library chooses three possible consultants. Once a consultant has been agreed upon, the Society contacts the consultant, facilitates his or her visit, sets standards for the consultant's written report, reviews findings and reports the findings to the institution. Applications for the service and information about the consultants participating in the program are available from the Society.

Screening Employees

It is wise for employers to carefully scrutinize all prospective emloyees or anyone gaining access to archives. John Kinney proves that such care has not always been taken. A few years after a Texas theft ring was broken up, one of the members "applied for the position of archivist in a large Texas library and was being seriously considered for the position at the time of his arrest in Saltillo, Mexico, on document theft charges."[34] The SAA suggests that "all repository employees who handle valuable manuscripts should be bonded under a theft insurance plan."[35]

The campus police at the University of Missouri have suggested that bonding of employees, an accepted risk-management principle, is appropriate for staff members in a manuscript repository.[36]

Importance of Record Keeping

A complete record of holdings is essential both for taking inventory and for proving ownership of valuable materials. Insufficiency of records makes theft all the more tempting. As Christopher C. Jaeckel points out, one library's practice of noting only the number of items in a file is particularly dangerous. "What," he asks, "is to prevent someone from replacing a letter with a steel engraving. . .? The library still has its . . . items, the thief has a fine new acquisition. . . ."[37]

Proper records are vital not only to keeping materials but to securing their return as well. After one book collector suspected that letters by Hamilton, Jefferson and Madison worth $20,000 were library property, state archivists had difficulty proving ownership. Eventually the library proved ownership by obtaining photocopies of interlibrary loan records.[38]

Strict Access Rules

Many institutions have strict rules on who is admitted to archives. Wayne State University allows janitorial and maintenance staff in archives only during regular working hours and under staff supervision. Access is similarly restricted for campus security officers.

Some institutions require two pieces of identification before an outsider is admitted to archives. The American Antiquarian Society conducts an interview with prospective users and requires references or faculty endorsements, while the North Carolina Division of Archives and History admits only users with photo-identification cards. IDs are obtained from a security officer after the patron has presented suitable identification. The card is surrendered at the reference desk and remains with the call slips completed by the user. Several institutions use inkless thumb printing as a protection against false identification cards. The patron presses his right thumb first on a colorless ink pad and then on a special sticker that is affixed to the back of his registration card.[39]

Checking identification is essential. One Robert Bradford Murphy passed himself off as Dr. Bradford, historian and consultant in Western history for the Library of Congress, to the Georgia Department of Archives and History; as R.O. Stanhope, journalist, to the Indiana State Library; as Dr. Murphy, journalist residing in Illinois, to the National Archives. When arrested in 1963, Murphy was found with six suitcases crammed with historical manuscripts and rare books and with receipts for 10 cartons of books shipped to Chicago.[40]

Archive Regulations

Archives should supply researchers with written rules governing use. A copy should be signed by the user and kept on file. A common practice is not to allow briefcases and coats in the reading room. The manuscript division of the Library of Congress provides lockers and facilities for such items. Some repositories require researchers to sign a consent form agreeing to a personal search when they leave the library. Discreet signs should be posted to this effect.

Surveillance

To check on researchers using archives, personal supervision, two-way mirrors and closed-circuit television can be used. The famous Mr. Murphy did most of his pilfering from the National Archives during evening hours, when two archivists had to service a large reading room. The SAA security manual suggests that "the tables in the reading room be arranged so that all patrons are clearly visible from the reference desk."[41]

Another obvious measure is to limit and monitor entrances. The American Antiquarian Society has a guard-receptionist on duty.

Timothy Walch, associate director of the SAA Archival Security Program, says, "Vigilant reference room surveillance is the nucleus of an effective library security program."[42]

Marking Manuscripts

Marking manuscripts can be a costly, time-consuming project; however, the most valuable items should be marked. William F.E. Morley discusses the potential of introducing a 3M product, microtaggants—tiny, invisible multilayered particles that can be processed to over half a million different layer combinations—for manuscript marking. However, the four most common methods of marking manuscripts are embossing, perforating, using invisible ink and using indelible ink.[43] The consensus is that indelible ink is preferable. The Library of Congress has developed and tested an ink for manuscripts that is nonacidic, nonbleeding, nonfading and indelible. A free bottle is available in blue, black or brown by writing to the office of the Assistant Director of Preservation, Library of Congress, Washington, DC 20540.

Libraries failing to mark valuable items have paid heavily for this omission. A 15th century manuscript from Queens College Library ended up for sale in a Swiss antiquarian bookshop.[44] The patron who borrowed it died and his library was sold. The manuscript was unmarked and, therefore, sold with the borrower's other books.

Microfilming

Microfilming is a simple precautionary way of protecting valuable materials. The SAA suggests that either particularly valuable materials be removed from collections and replaced with photocopies or the entire collection be microfilmed, especially when there are so many valuable items that separation becomes impractical.[45]

In October 1962 staff members at the National Archives noticed that nine folders of letters were missing from the Attorney General's files. Fortunately a Stanford University professor had microfilmed much of the file a few months prior to its disappearance.[46] Microfilm prevents defacement and permits valuable items to be stored in vaults; if marked documents are microfilmed, the film is additional proof that the manuscripts are library property.

Inventory, Access Logs, Locks

Other security measures include taking regular inventories of valuable items and maintaining complete access logs and records of use.

The Society of American Archivists also suggests that libraries should not hesitate to report thefts and to prosecute thieves. Librarians are also urged to call police officials if they suspect a possible theft, so that the police know how to respond when their assistance is needed.

Even the matter of door locks should not be overlooked. Among the recommendations of experts are "locks with case-hardened centers, five-tumbler cylinders, and one-and-a-half-inch dead bolts." Additional precautions are suggested for doors with exterior hinges.[47]

CONCLUSION

The basic theft-prevention measures outlined in this chapter are the result of painful, costly experience. Whether employed separately or together, security measures such as restricted access, discreet employee screening, microfilming, manuscript marking and co-operation with law-enforcement officers are essential to security planning. Library consultant Raymond Holt insists that this planning "must be recognized as a continuing part of the library's operations."[48]

FOOTNOTES

1. Pamela Bluh, "A Study of an Inventory," *Library Resources and Technical Services,* Summer 1969, p. 368.

2. "Security in Libraries," *Library Journal,* June 1, 1979, p. 1206.

3. "Mutilation in the Young Adult Section," *Library Security Newsletter,* Spring 1976, p. 5.

4. J.W. Griffith, "Library Thefts: A Problem That Won't Go Away," *American Libraries,* April 1978, pp. 224-27.

5. G.H. Souter, "Delinquent Readers: A Study of the Problem in University Libraries," *Journal of Librarianship,* April 1976, p. 101.

6. Griffith, *op. cit.,* p. 227.

7. "Perspiring Periodicals Thief," *American Libraries,* March 1972, p. 228.

8. "Mail Box," *AB Bookman's Weekly,* December 6, 1971, p. 1756.

9. "The Worse They Get," *Wilson Library Bulletin,* November 1976, p. 217.

10. "Periodical Theft/Mutilation Reported to be Relieved by Microform Conversion," *Library Security Newsletter,* Spring 1976, p. 20.

11. "Mutilation," *op. cit.,* p. 5.

12. "Preventive Medicine," *Library Journal,* July 1977, p. 1447.

13. Eugene Garfield, "Highly Cited Articles: Human Psychology and Behavior," *Current Contents (Social and Behavioral Science),* Vol. 7, No. 18, 1975, pp. 5-11.

14. Marjorie E. Murfin and Clyde Hendrick, "Ripoffs Tell Their Story," *The Journal of Academic Librarianship,* May 1975, p. 10.

15. Herbert Katzenstein, "Guidelines for Security of AV Equipment," *Library Security Newsletter,* July 1975, p. 9.

16. "Art Works Stolen from Two New England Libraries," *Library Journal,* September 15, 1975, p. 1592.

17. Nancy H. Knight, "Theft Detection Systems Revisited: An Updated Survey," *Library Technology Reports,* May/June 1979, p. 339.

18. "$500 Fines at CPL," *Library Journal,* August 1979, p. 1510.

19. "Security in Libraries," *Library Journal,* April 15, 1979, p. 878.

20. Brooke Anson, "Foil That Audiovisual Thief," *Wisconsin Library Bulletin,* July 1978, p. 168.

21. Patricia McCarthy, "They Shelved Media Openly," *Wisconsin Library Bulletin,* January-February 1976, p. 30.

22. Katzenstein, *op. cit.,* p. 9.

23. "Sorry, Wrong Number," *Library Security Newsletter,* March 1975, p. 11.

24. Evelyn Samuel, "Protection of Library and Archival Materials," *Library and Archival Security,* Vol. 2, No. 3/4, 1978, p. 5.

25. Philip P. Mason, "Archival Security: New Solutions to an Old Problem," *The American Archivist,* October 1975, p. 480.

26. "Book Theft Control Follows Museum Loss," *Library Journal,* October 1, 1972, p. 3108.

27. "New Mexico University Library: Site of Book Heist," *Library Journal,* June 15, 1973, p. 1866.

28. Mason, *op. cit.,* p. 477.

29. "Music Scores Stolen from Pittsburgh's Carnegie," *Library Journal,* July 1977, p. 1447.

30. "Yale and Newberry Recover Stolen Maps," *American Libraries,* March 1979, p. 100.

31. Antiquarian Booksellers' Association, *Book Thefts from Libraries* (London: Antiquarian Booksellers' Association, 972).

32. John M. Kinney, "Archival Security and Insecurity," *The American Archivist,* October 1975, p. 493.

33. For missing volumes that do not fit into these categories, *Bookman's Weekly* has added a special section to its classified pages to list books missing from libraries, shops and individual collections. The fee is $1.00 per line. Descriptions should be sent to *Bookman's Weekly,* PO Box BW, Clifton, NJ 07015.

34. Kinney, *op. cit.,* pp. 494, 495.

35. Timothy Walch, *Archives and Manuscripts: Security* (Basic Manual Series) (Chicago: Society of American Archivists 1977), p. 5.

36. "Archival Security Surveys," *Archival Security Newsletter,* July 1976, p. 6.

37. Christopher C. Jaeckel, "Manuscripts: Growing Problem of Thefts," *AB Bookman's Weekly,* May 21, 1979, p. 3858.

38. Walch, *op. cit.,* p. 1.

39. *Ibid.,* p. 6.

40. Mason, *op. cit.,* p. 485.

41. Walch, *op. cit.,* p. 6.

42. Timothy Walch, "The Improvement of Library Security," *College and Research Libraries,* March 1977, p. 102.

43. William F.E. Morley, "Security or Defacement," *Canadian Library Journal,* December 1978, p. 424.

44. Antiquarian Booksellers' Association, *op. cit.,* pp. 8, 9.

45. Walch, *op. cit.,* p. 8.

46. Mason, *op. cit.,* p. 484.

47. "Door Locks and Archival Security," *Archival Security Newsletter,* January 1977, n.p.

48. Raymond L. Holt, "Commentary," *Library Security Newsletter,* September-October 1975, pp. 7-8.

VIII

Summary and Conclusions

More than 10 years ago the retired director of the Free Library of Philadelphia, Emerson Greenaway, wrote: "Prevention of book thefts is one of the most urgent problems facing our library and others."[1] His comment still holds true, for reports of massive thefts are ongoing:

- In 1975 a New York attorney was indicted for taking 15,000 books, worth $125,000, from the New York Public Library.[2]

- In 1976 a Stanford University student admitted stealing $100,000 worth of rare books from the University's library.[3]

- In 1978 10,000 library books were found in the flat of a couple evicted from a building in Hove, East Sussex, England.[4]

- In 1979 Gervase Chesire, an English instructor at the University of California at Riverside, was arraigned for the theft of more than 10,000 books. The estimated cost of the stolen materials, many of which were taken to the San Bernardino and Riverside dumps, where they were watered down and covered with garbage, was between $100,000 and $200,000.[5]

Of perhaps even greater consequence is the ongoing decimation of library collections by numerous users, which sometimes results in loss figures exceeding 30% of the collection. According to Donald E. Wright, librarian at the Evanston (IL) Public Library, "The largest percentage of stops with our electronic security system is with an ordinary patron, the run-of-the-mill patron who proclaims a multitude of excuses for taking library materials, ranging from 'I forgot my library card' to 'I needed a longer loan period.'" As is pointed out in Chapter I, even a 1% annual loss rate means U.S. libraries are losing 15 million volumes a year.

CALCULATING LOSSES

What is a library to do? First, the extent and kind of loss must be determined. To determine the extent of loss, libraries have relied on the book census, the inventory and the sample, all discussed in Chapter II. Whereas any gauge of loss is useful, annual loss figures are the best type. They indicate what the library loses currently, whether a security program is needed and how much the library can afford to spend on such a program. To determine the kind of loss, libraries analyze inventory and sample data to isolate high-loss areas—audiovisual materials rather than monographs, 300s rather than 800s. Only after a library identifies the nature of its losses can it choose a security program that is designed to curtail those particular losses.

If the bulk of collection loss can be attributed to unreturned materials (overdues), for example, an electronic security system will not reduce loss. Neither will closed-circuit television surveillance or staff patrols. If high losses are sustained in only one or two subject areas, the library might consider closed stacks for those subject areas only, or it might ensure that professors in those subject areas put high-demand materials on reserve, or it might buy an electronic security system and reduce system software costs by inserting targets primarily in materials concerning those one or two subjects. If the majority of losses are serials, converting to microform might eliminate the problem. Another alternative is to place serials behind the circulation desk—closing stacks, in effect, but minimizing the need for additional staff by using circulation attendants to retrieve needed periodical volumes.

LEARNING FROM RETAILERS

Libraries can learn several lessons from retailers. Annual inventories at the University of Utah Bookstore indicated that clothing and paper supplies were hardly ever stolen. What students resented most was the spiraling cost of textbooks, and it was those materials that accounted for most of the store's shrinkage (inventory loss). When the store installed a 3M book theft detection system, therefore, personnel targeted books only. Most retailers secure their buildings. Mall-type stores, for example, often have no windows. Many library books have been lost through open windows. No electronic security system could reduce such losses, but libraries might install mesh screens or locks on some windows. Moreover, large bookstore chains know that losses are higher in some locations than in others— center-city stores lose more than suburban ones. No chain would install electronic systems in all branches; neither should a library. Effective solutions to a theft problem require careful study not only of available systems but of the extent and pattern of losses. Large bookstore chains study alternatives and losses for years before investing staff time and funds to security programs. Libraries should not hesitate to do the same.

SECURITY MEASURES

What are the options? There are guards, stack patrols, closed stacks, tighter circulation control, amnesty programs and special in-house security techniques. Most of these are discussed in Chapter VI. The increasingly popular solution, however, is electronic security. At present there are four major electronic security system vendors with library installations: 3M, Checkpoint, Knogo and Gaylord. Gaylord will unveil its second-generation system in early 1981. Sentronic is making design modifications, but is not yet a major competitor. Breaking ground in the library security market are LPS and Sensormatic, long the largest vendor of retail security systems. LPS has one library installation, but is pursuing retail franchises much more actively. Sensormatic began testing a new magnetic system in September 1980. If all goes well, librarians will have yet another system from which to choose.

All electronic security systems operate in much the same way. Vendors provide targets, sensitized (specially treated) tags or strips, that are to be affixed to library materials and must be desensitized during checkout procedures. All systems also include sensing screens: units that electronically or magnetically search for the presence of sensitized targets as patrons exit through the screens. They signal a series of alarms if targets are detected. Finally, with the exception of Checkpoint, which employs specially treated date due cards to shield targets, the systems provide a variety of hardware to sensitize and desensitize targets. Installation is an uncomplicated process if the library building is already fairly secure and if its design is not unduly complex. Most systems require only proper, dedicated wiring. After their first year of operation, service contracts are available. The main difference between systems is their operating principle: radio frequency, electromagnetism and magnetism. Chapter III describes available systems, their similarities and their differences.

LIMITATIONS OF ELECTRONIC SYSTEMS

Interviews with users of electronic security systems, reported in Chapter V, indicate that while all systems reduce loss, there is some dissatisfaction with false alarms, service and, in some cases, software—its adhesiveness, availability and price. Such systems are not foolproof; they are between 75% and 95% effective. Guards and amnesty programs, though not as fully studied as electronic security systems, often seem to be equally effective. In fact, any noticeable effort by the library to reduce theft serves as an effective deterrent. Retailers and librarians alike attribute the success of electronic security in part to its deterrent ability, as well as its ability to forestall a theft in progress. The presence of any system makes clientele and patrons aware that the institution or establishment is doing something about theft.

Besides understanding that electronic security systems will not completely prevent theft, librarians should realize that these systems offer no protection for rare books. Target application would be difficult and might damage materials. These problems are discussed in Chapter VII. Fortunately, organized professional activity in this field has established a network of information and assistance. The Society of American Archivists, for instance, publishes a list of valuable missing materials and also offers a security consultant service to small archives for a modest price.

Moreover, the sensitize-desensitize units of electronic security systems should not be in close proximity to cathode ray tubes (CRTs). If the library has or plans to acquire an automated circulation system, therefore, a little extra thought about CRT and sensitize-desensitize placement is necessary to assure that CRTs do not inhibit the effective functioning of the electronic security system. Aware that librarians would like interfaces between automated circulation and electronic security systems, vendors have worked to develop them. At the University of Texas at Dallas, for example, the entire check-out procedure, including discharge and desensitization, is automatic. That system uses a 3M book theft detection system. Cincinnati Electronics has designed an interface between its automated circulation system, CLASSIC, and Checkpoint models. A few years ago Knogo planned to wed its security system with a circulation system produced by Automated Library Systems, an English firm. Though plans fell through, ALS has interfaced both systems in one European library.

THE ROLE OF LIBRARY STAFF

Knowing the limitations as well as the special features of available systems helps the library determine the security program or programs most compatible with its long-range goals, philosophy of service, budget, and staff and collection size. That compatibility goes a long way toward ensuring staff cooperation—a prerequisite to the effectiveness of any system. A staff that believes in neither the necessity for nor the effectiveness of a stack patrol or an electronic security system assures the failure of such a program.

Accelerating library thefts should be expected over the next few years. Higher book prices and rising tuition costs make library collections especially vulnerable. From the library's point of view, however, book theft and shrinking budgets make security measures increasingly necessary. Communication between the library and its patrons is vital. Studies show that when patrons realize what theft costs them (the use of books they needed or wanted) and what it costs the library (sometimes 50% more than the work's original purchase and processing cost)—as well as how difficult, if not impossible, it is to replace certain titles—they are less likely to steal. The job of informing the public rests with the library staff.

Solving the costly and difficult problem of collection loss is a painstaking process, and there are no shortcuts. A dedicated, informed, security-conscious staff, however, will contribute greatly to the success of any security program.

FOOTNOTES

1. "To Test Book Theft Prevention," *American Library Association Bulletin,* April 1968, p. 337.
2. "Book Theft on the Upswing," *Library Journal,* December 1, 1975, p. 2203.
3. "Stanford's Book Heist," *Library Journal,* December 1, 1976, p. 2418.
4. "10,000 Stolen Books Found," *Library Association Record,* June 1978, p. 266.
5. "Grand Larceny," *Wilson Library Bulletin,* May 1979, p. 617.

Appendix I

The Mississippi Library Materials Security Act

Mississippi State Legislature
1978

> An Act Creating Offenses Relating to Libraries, Archives
> and Other Depositories; to Establish Penalties; and for
> Related Purposes

BE IT ENACTED BY THE LEGISLATURE OF THE STATE OF MISSISSIPPI:

SECTION 1.   This act shall be known and may be cited as the "Mississippi Library Materials Security Act."

SECTION 2.   (1) It shall be unlawful for any person to remove library materials, without authorization, from the premises wherein such materials are maintained or to retain possession of library materials without authorization.

(2) It shall be unlawful for any person to willfully mutilate library materials.

SECTION 3.   As used in this act the term:

(a) "Without authorization" means contrary to rules which set forth policies governing access to library materials and include eligibility for library patronage and lending procedures.

(b) "Library materials" means books, manuscripts, letters, newspapers, court records, films, microfilms, tape recordings, phonograph records, lithographs, prints, photographs or any other written or printed document, graphic material of any nature and other personal property which is the property or in the custody of or entrusted to a public or private library, museum, archives or other depository.

(c) "Mutilate" means, in addition to its commonly accepted definition, the willful removal or separation of constituent parts of an item of library materials, causing library materials to be exposed to damage; or duplication without authorization.

SECTION 4.   The provisions of this act shall apply to all libraries, museums, archives and other depositories operated by an agency, board, commission, department or officer of the State of Mississippi, by private persons, societies or organizations, or by agencies or officers of municipalities, counties, school and junior college districts or of any other political subdivisions of the State of Mississippi.

SECTION 5.   Any person who violates the provisions of Section 2 of this act is guilty of a misdemeanor and shall be punished by a fine not to exceed Five Hundred Dollars ($500.00) or by imprisonment in the county jail not to exceed six (6) months, or by both such fine and imprisonment.

SECTION 6.   The provisions of this act are supplemental to other criminal statutes. An acquittal or conviction obtained under this act shall not be a bar to civil proceedings or actions arising from the same incident.

SECTION 7.   Any person employed by a library or any person charged with the supervision thereof with reason to believe that any person has committed or has attempted to commit any offense defined in Section 2 of this act, or if any person is believed to have concealed upon his person or within his belongings any library material, such person may be detained and questioned in a reasonable manner for the purpose of ascertaining whether or not such offense has been committed. Such detention and questioning shall not render such employee civilly liable for slander, false arrest, false imprisonment, malicious prosecution, unlawful detention or otherwise in any case where such library employee acts in good faith and in a reasonable manner.

SECTION 8.   This act shall take effect and be in force from and after July 1, 1978.

Reprinted with the permission of the Mississippi Library Association from *Mississippi Library News,* 42: 75 + (June 1978).

Appendix II

Libraries Using Electronic Security Systems

CHECKPOINT SYSTEMS

Checkpoint Systems: Mark II and Mark III are installed and operational in the following representative library locations (partial list):

Public Libraries

Arlington Heights Memorial Library, Arlington Heights, IL
Bellingham Public Library, Bellingham, WA
Broadview Public Library, Broadview, IL
Brooklyn Public Library, Flatlands Branch, Brooklyn, NY
Cedarburg Public Library, Cedarburg, WI
Charleston County Library, Charleston, SC
Eau Claire Public Library, Eau Claire, WI
Elmont Public Library, Elmont, NY
El Paso Public Library, El Paso, TX
Garden City Public Library, Garden City, MI
Greensboro Public Library, Greensboro, NC
Hennepin County Library, Southdale Branch, Edina, MN
Huntsville Public Library, Huntsville, AL
Indian River County Library, Vero Beach, FL
James V. Brown Library, Williamsport, PA
Janesville Public Library, Janesville, WI
La Crosse Public Library, La Crosse, WI
Lewis & Clark Public Library, Helena, MT
Milwaukee Public Library, Milwaukee, WI
Mississauga Public Library, Mississauga, Ontario, Canada
North York Public Library, Downsview Area, Ontario, Canada
Oakland Public Library, Oakland, CA
Oak Park Public Library, Oak Park, IL
Oshkosh Public Library, Oshkosh, WI

Parkersburg and Wood County Public Library, Parkersburg, WV
Penrose Public Library, Colorado Springs, CO
Public Library of Cincinnati & Hamilton County, Cincinnati, OH
Reading Public Library, Reading, MA
San Mateo Public Library, San Mateo, CA
Santa Monica Public Library, Santa Monica, CA
Seattle Public Library, Seattle, WA
Worcester Public Library, Worcester, MA

College and University Libraries

American University, Washington, DC
Beloit College, Beloit, WI
College of Insurance, New York, NY
Concordia Seminary, St. Louis, MO
Dartmouth College, Hanover, NH
D'Youville College—Library Resources Center, Buffalo, NY
George Washington University, Washington, DC
Gettysburg College, Gettysburg, PA
Hampton Institute, Hampton, VA
Holy Family College, Philadelphia, PA
La Salle College, Philadelphia, PA
Lycoming College, Williamsport, PA
Lynchburg College, Lynchburg, VA
Marymount College of Kansas, Salina, KS
National University, San Diego, CA
Northeastern Oklahoma State University, Tahlequah, OK
Pace University College of White Plains, White Plains, NY
Pennsylvania State University Libraries, University Park, PA
Pennsylvania State University
        Physical Sciences Library, University Park, PA
        Worthington Scranton Campus, Dunmore, PA
Ricks College—David O. McKay Learning Resources Center, Rexburg, ID
Springfield College, Springfield, MA
State University of New York at Utica-Rome, Utica, NY
Suffolk University, Boston, MA
University of Connecticut, Storrs, CT
University of Delaware, Newark, DE
University of Pennsylvania, Philadelphia, PA
University of Puget Sound, Tacoma, WA
University of South Carolina, Thomas Cooper Library, Columbia, SC
University of Texas at El Paso, El Paso, TX
University of Wisconsin, Engineering & Physical Sciences Library, Madison, WI
Columbia Basin College, Pasco, WA
Atlantic Community College, Mays Landing, NJ
North Seattle Community College, Seattle, WA
Antelope Valley College, Lancaster, CA
CEGEP de Valleyfield, Valleyfield, Quebec, Canada
Los Angeles Community College District (8 colleges) Los Angeles, CA
Linn-Benton Community College, Albany, OR
Pensacola Junior College, Pensacola, FL

Grand Rapids Junior College, Grand Rapids, MI
Modesto Junior College, Modesto, CA
Morton College, Cicero, IL
Northeast Alabama State Junior College, Rainsville, AL
Bristol Community College, Fall River, MA
J. Sargeant Reynolds Community College, Downtown and Parham Campuses,
    Richmond, VA
Tarrant County Junior College, Northwest Campus, Fort Worth, TX

High School Libraries

Roseville High School, Roseville, CA
Bradley-Bourbonnais Comm. High School, Bradley, IL
Roberto Clemente High School, Chicago, IL
Niles High School North, Skokie, IL
Pontiac Northern High School, Pontiac, MI
Westfield High School, Westfield, NJ
Kettering Fairmont West High School, Kettering, OH
Sir Robert Borden High School, Ottawa, Ontario, Canada
Fremont Unified High School District, Sunnyvale, CA
West Ferris Secondary School, North Bay, Ontario, Canada
Connellsville Senior High School, Connellsville, PA
Livermore High School, Livermore, CA
Lyons Township High School, LaGrange, IL
Fenton High School, Bensonville, IL
Great Valley Senior High School, Malvern, PA
Bothell High School, Bothell, WA
Issaquah High School, Issaquah, WA
Curtis High School, West Tacoma, WA
Hempfield High School, Greensburg, PA
Valley Forge Senior High School, Parma, OH
Lamphere Public Schools, Madison Heights, MI
L.W. Higgins High School, Marrero, LA
Sonora Union High School, Sonora, CA
Lenape High School, Medford, NJ
York County Vocational Technical School, York, PA
Taft School, Watertown, CT
Yonkers High School, Yonkers, NY
Inglemoor High School, Bothell, WA
East High School, Phoenix, AZ
Meridian High School, North Campus, Meridian, MS
Bedford High School, Resource Center, Bedford, OH

Special Libraries

Pennsylvania State University Engineering Library, University Park, PA
Stanford University Lane Medical Library, Palo Alto, CA
District One Technical Institute, Eau Claire, WI
Columbia University Health Sciences Library, New York, NY
University of Texas Health Science Center at San Antonio, San Antonio, TX
New England College of Optometry, Boston, MA

Northwestern University Medical, Chicago, IL
University of Nebraska Medical Center, Omaha, NE
University of South Carolina Coleman Karesh Law Library, Columbia, SC
St. Louis University Law Library, St. Louis, MO
University of Arkansas for Medical Sciences, Little Rock, AR
Medical College of Ohio at Toledo, Raymond H. Mulford Medical Library, Toledo, OH
University of Rochester, Eastman School of Music, Rochester, NY
Northwestern University Dental School Library, Chicago, IL
Wright State University School of Medicine-Health Sciences Library, Dayton, OH
University of Colorado Medical Center, Denison Memorial Library, Denver, CO
Washington-Holmes Area Vocational-Tech. Center, Chipley, FL
Wesley Medical Center, Hospital Library, Wichita, KS
Brigham Young University, J. Reuben Clark Law Library, Provo, UT
Northeast Wisconsin VTAE District, Green Bay, WI
Florida State University Law Library, Tallahassee, FL

GAYLORD LIBRARY SYSTEMS

Gaylord/Magnavox Book Security Systems are installed and operational in the following representative library locations (partial list):

Public Libraries

Addison Public Library, Addison, IL
Allentown Public Library, Allentown, PA
Arlington Public Library, Arlington, TX
Aurora Public Library, Aurora, CO
Bethlehem Public Library, Bethlehem, PA
Prince Georges Memorial Library—Bowie Branch, Bowie, MD
Burlingame Public Library, Burlingame, CA
Chula Vista Public Library, Chula Vista, CA
Commack Public Library, Commack, NY
Fairlawn Public Library, Fairlawn, NJ
Irving Public Library, Irving, TX
Largo Public Library, Largo, FL
Prince Georges Memorial Library—New Carrollton Branch, New Carrollton, MD
Oak Lawn Public Library, Oak Lawn, IL
Metropolitan Library System, Oklahoma City, OK
     Ralph Ellison Branch Library
Park Forest Public Library, Park Forest, IL
Port Jefferson Public Library, Port Jefferson, NY
Comsewogue Public Library, Port Jefferson Station, NY
Puyallup Public Library, Puyallup, WA
Santa Fe Public Library, Santa Fe, NM
Martin Memorial Library, York, PA

College and University Libraries

Siena Heights College, Adrian, MI

Allentown College, Center Valley, PA
St. Xavier College, Chicago, IL
University of Miami Law Library, Coral Gables, FL
Misericordia College, Dallas, PA
Delaware Valley College, Doylestown, PA
Francis Marion College, Florence, SC
Broward Community College—Central Campus, Fort Lauderdale, FL
Carroll College, Helena, MT
South Texas College of Law, Houston, TX
Kilgore College, Kilgore, TX
Oscar Rose Junior College, Midwest City, OK
Broward Community College—North Campus, Pompano Beach, FL
St. Clair Community College, Port Huron, MI
Eastern New Mexico University, Roswell, NM
College of the Virgin Islands, St. Thomas, VI
Syracuse University, E.S. Bird Library, Syracuse, NY
Syracuse University, Engineering & Life Sciences Library, Syracuse, NY
Bentley College, Waltham, MA
Western Maryland College, Westminster, MD

High School Libraries

Gateway High School, Aurora, CO
Commodore Middle School, Bainbridge Island, WA
Conestoga Senior High School, Berwyn, PA
Benedictine High School, Cleveland, OH
St. Ignatius High School, Cleveland, OH
Bensalem High School, Cornwell Heights, PA
East Lansing High School, East Lansing, MI
West Valley High School, Fairbanks, AK
South Florence High School, Florence, SC
West Florence High School, Florence, SC
Irvine High School, Irvine, CA
Irving High School, Irving, TX
MacArthur High School, Irving, TX
Nimitz High School, Irving, TX
Harmon Senior High School, Kansas City, KS
Schlagle Senior High School, Kansas City, KS
Sumner Senior High School, Kansas City, KS
Washington Senior High School, Kansas City, KS
Wyandotte Senior High School, Kansas City, KS
Hickman Mills High School, Kansas City, MO
Ruskin High School, Kansas City, MO
Longbranch Junior-Senior High School, Longbranch, NJ
Denbigh High School, Newport News, VA
Ferguson High School, Newport News, VA
Menchville Senior High School, Newport News, VA
Lincoln-Sudbury Regional High School, Sudbury, MA
Lincoln High School, Tacoma, WA
Columbia River High School, Vancouver, WA

Fort Vancouver High School, Vancouver, WA
Hudson's Bay High School, Vancouver, WA
Bainbridge Island High School, Winslow, WA

Special Libraries

Fort Lewis Library, Fort Lewis, WA
St. Vincent's Hospital Medical Library, New York, NY

KNOGO CORP.

Knogo Mark IV security systems are installed and operational in the following representative library locations (complete list):

Public Libraries

Hicksville Public Library, Hicksville, NY
Freeport Public Library, Freeport, NY
New Orleans Public Library, New Orleans, LA
New Bedford Public Library, New Bedford, MA
Palmdale Public Library, Palmdale, CA
Silas Bronson Library, Waterbury, CT
Clark County Public Library, Las Vegas, NV
Long Beach Public Library, Long Beach, NY
Plainview-Old Bethpage Public Library, Plainview, NY
Evanston Public Library, Evanston, IL
Groton Public Library, Groton, CT
Calgary Public Library, Calgary, Alberta, Canada
Rosenberg Library, Galveston, TX
Oakville Public Library, Oakville, Ontario, Canada
Roseville Public Library, Roseville, CA
Torrance Public Library, Torrance, CA
Highland Park Public Library, Highland Park, IL
Torrington Library, Torrington, CT
Marin County Library, San Rafael, CA
The Dalles Public Library, The Dalles, OR
Mesa County Public Library, Grand Junction, CO
Glenview Public Library, Glenview, IL
Charleston Heights Library—Clark County Arts Center, Las Vegas, NV
Beloit Public Library, Beloit, WI
East Brunswick Public Library, East Brunswick, NJ

College and University Libraries

Ole Miss Law Library, University of Mississippi, Oxford, MS
Ole Miss Main Library, University of Mississippi, Oxford, MS
New River Community College, Dublin, VA
Brookdale Community College, Lincroft, NJ
University of Calgary, Calgary, Alberta, Canada
Lamar University, Beaumont, TX
University of St. Thomas, Houston, TX

State University of New York Agricultural & Technical College, Alfred, NY
Mississippi Gulf Coast Jr. College, Perkinston, MS
Texas Women's College, Dallas, TX
University of Calgary Medical School, Calgary, Alberta, Canada
Arizona State University, Tempe, AZ
Hampshire College, Amherst, MA
Victor Valley Community College, Victorville, CA
Hebrew Union College, New York, NY
University of Hartford, Hartford, CT
Fort Valley State College, Fort Valley, GA
Nicholls State University, Thibodaux, LA
Medicine Hat College, Medicine Hat, Alberta, Canada
University of Hawaii, Honolulu, HI
 Hamilton Library
 Sinclair Library
North Country Community College, Saranac Lake, NY
Texas A & M, College Station, TX
Texas Woman's University, Dallas, TX
University of Massachusetts, Amherst, MA
 Main Library
 Physical Sciences Library
Bard College, Annandale-on-Hudson, NY
Princeton University—Firestone Library, Princeton, NJ
Sarah Lawrence College, Bronxville, NY
North Texas State University, Denton, TX
 Main Library
 Information Science Library
Trinity College, Hartford, CT
Riverside City College, Riverside, CA
New York Institute of Technology, New York, NY
Cumberland County Community College, Vineland, NJ
City University of New York, The Graduate Center, New York, NY
University of Houston, Clear Lake City, TX
Thornton Community College, South Holland, IL
Napa Valley Community College, Napa, CA
Amherst College—Frost Library, Amherst, MA
Central Arizona College, Coolidge, AZ
New York Institute of Technology, Old Westbury, NY
 Main Library
 Education Library
University of Texas Medical School, Galveston, TX
Marshall University, Huntington, WV
Smith College, Northampton, MA
Mercer County Community College, Trenton, NJ
Clark County Community College, Las Vegas, NV
Virginia Highlands Community College, Abingdon, VA
University of Alabama, Tuscaloosa, AL
 Main Library
 Business Library
 Education Library
 Engineering Library
 Science Library

Marshall University Medical School, Huntington, WV
American River College, Sacramento, CA
Kingsborough Community College, Brooklyn, NY
Catholic University—Music Library, Washington, DC
University of Wisconsin, Whitewater, WI

High School Libraries

Bonanza High School, Las Vegas, NV
Norwalk High School, Norwalk, CT
Soquel High School, Soquel, CA
El Dorado High School, Placerville, CA
Sutton High School, Sutton West, Ontario, Canada
Wilson High School, San Francisco, CA
O'Connell High School, San Francisco, CA
Burbank Junior High School, San Francisco, CA
Presidio Junior High School, San Francisco, CA
Benjamin Franklin Junior High School, San Francisco, CA
Gunn High School, Palo Alto, CA
Horace Mann Junior High School, San Francisco, CA
Galileo High School, San Francisco, CA
J. Lick Junior High School, San Francisco, CA
J. Denman Junior High School, San Francisco, CA
Amity Regional High School, Woodbridge, CT
El Cerrito High School, El Cerrito, CA
Bryant High School, Long Island City, NY
Syosset High School, Syosset, NY
Winsted High School, Winsted, CT
Sturgeon High School, Morinville, Alberta, Canada
Ponderosa High School, Shingle Springs, CA
Aptos Junior High School, San Francisco, CA
Herbert Hoover Junior High School, San Francisco, CA
Everett Junior High School, San Francisco, CA
Giannini Junior High School, San Francisco, CA
Jefferson Union High School, Daly City, CA
Lowell High School, San Francisco, CA
Marina High School, San Francisco, CA
Balboa High School, San Francisco, CA
V. Valley Junior High School, San Francisco, CA
Pelton Junior High School, San Francisco, CA
Francisco High School, San Francisco, CA
Kennedy High School, Richmond, CA
Lord Elgin High School, Burlington, Ontario, Canada
M.M. Robinson High School, Burlington, Ontario, Canada
Burlington Central High School, Burlington, Ontario, Canada
Georgetown District High School, Georgetown, Ontario, Canada
Mission High School, San Francisco, CA
Roosevelt Junior High School, San Francisco, CA
Torrington High School, Torrington, CT
Palisades High School, Los Angeles, CA
Rocky River High School, Rocky River, OH

Newington High School, Newington, CT
McNary High School, Salem, OR
Owosso High School, Owosso, MI
Weston High School, Weston, CT
Gilroy High School, Gilroy, CA
Hollywood High School, Los Angeles, CA
Belmont High School, Los Angeles, CA
El Camino Real High School, Woodland Hills, CA
Wayne Memorial High School, Wayne, MI
Potrero Junior High School, San Francisco, CA
Great Neck North High School, Great Neck, NY
Piedmont High School, Piedmont, CA
De La Salle High School, Concord, CA
John Glenn High School, Westland, MI
North Thurston District No. 3, Lacy, WA
Madison Senior High School, Rochester, NY
Franklin Junior-Senior High School, Rochester, NY
Monroe Junior-Senior High School, Rochester, NY
Marshfield High School, Coos Bay, OR
North Penn School District, Lansdale, PA
David Crockett High School, Austin, TX
Blaine Senior High School, Coon Rapids, MI
Morro Bay High School, Morro Bay, CA
Roosevelt High School, Yonkers, NY
Orange Glenn High School, Escondido, CA

Special Libraries

Genealogical Library, Church of Jesus Christ Latter Day Saints, Salt Lake City, UT
Greenhaven Correctional Facility, Stormville, NY
HEW Law Research Library, Washington, DC

SENTRONIC INTERNATIONAL

Sentronic (Book-Mark) declined to provide a list of users; however, a search of the literature indicated the following libraries have installed either Sentronic or Book-Mark systems:

Public Libraries

Carnegie Public Library, Joplin, MO
Dayton Public Library, Dayton, OH
Flint Public Libraries, Flint, MI
Grand Rapids Public Library, Grand Rapids, MI
Hammond Public Library, Hammond, IN
Inglewood Public Library, Inglewood, CA
Joplin Public Library, Joplin, MO
Knox County Public Library, Knoxville, TN
Norwood Public Library, Norwood, MA

College and University Libraries

Bowling Green State University, Bowling Green, OH
Canal Zone College Library, Canal Zone, Panama
Case Western Reserve University, Cleveland, OH
Chabot College Library, Livermore, CA
Colegio Universitario Library, Caguas, PR
Curry College Library, Milton, MA
Eastern Michigan University Library, Ypsilanti, MI
Elmira College Library, Elmira, NY
Gordon College Library, Wenham, MA
Haile Sellassie I. University Library, Addis Ababa, Ethiopia
Indian Valley Community College Library, Novato, CA
Kentucky State College Library, Frankfort, KY
Laredo Junior College Library, Laredo, TX
Loyola Law School Library, New Orleans, LA
Miami-Dade Community College, Miami, FL
Mohawk Valley Community College Library, Utica, NY
Monroe Community College Library, Rochester, NY
Moraine Valley Community College Library, Palos Hills, IL
Ohio Wesleyan University Library, Delaware, OH
Pasadena City College Library, Pasadena, CA
Pepperdine University Library, Los Angeles, CA
Santa Barbara City College, Santa Barbara, CA
Staten Island Community College Library, Staten Island, NY
Terra Technical School Library, Fremont, OH
University of Kuwait Library, Kuwait
University of Texas Library, Odessa, TX
Westmont College Library, Santa Barbara, CA
Yuba Community College Library, Marysville, CA

High School Library

Swartz Creek Middle School, Swartz Creek, MI

Special Libraries

Ohio College of Podiatric Medicine Library, Cleveland, OH
Smithsonian Institution, National Museum of History and Technology, Washington, DC

3M CORP.

3M Corp.: Tattle-Tape and Spartan are installed and operational in more than 1500 libraries, including the following locations (partial list):

Public Libraries

Loussac Public Library, Anchorage, AK
Altadena Public Library, Altadena, CA
Beverly Hills Public Library, Beverly Hills, CA

Pasadena Public Library, Pasadena, CA
San Jose Public Library, San Jose, CA
Sunnyvale Public Library, Sunnyvale, CA
Whittier Public Library, Whittier, CA
Woodbridge Public Library, Woodbridge, CT
Greenwich Public Library, Greenwich, CT
Jacksonville Public Library, Jacksonville, FL
Brunswick Public Library, Brunswick, GA
Chicago Public Library, Woodson Regional Library, Chicago, IL
Davenport Public Library, Davenport, IA
Iowa City Public Library, Iowa City, IA
Brookline Public Library, Brookline, MA
Lansing Public Library, Lansing, MI
Brooklyn Public Library, Brooklyn, NY
Hempstead Public Library, Hempstead, NY
Islip Public Library, Islip, NY
Levittown Public Library, Levittown, NY
Wake County Public Library, Raleigh, NC
Eugene Public Library, Eugene, OR
Richland County Public Library, Columbia, SC
Greenville Public Library, Greenville, SC
Fort Worth Public Library, Fort Worth, TX
Norfolk Public Library, Norfolk, VA
Waynesboro Public Library, Waynesboro, VA

College and University Libraries

Pima College, Tucson, AZ
Claremont College, Claremont, CA
Glendale College, Glendale, CA
City College of San Francisco, San Francisco, CA
Arapahoe Community College, Littleton, CO
Trinidad State Jr. College, Trinidad, CO
Norwalk Community College, Norwalk, CT
Washington Technical Institute Library, Washington, DC
Daytona Beach Community College, Daytona Beach, FL
Santa Fe Community College, Gainesville, FL
Belleville Area College, Belleville, IL
Jefferson Community College, Louisville, KY
Morgan State College, Baltimore, MD
University of Maryland Baltimore County Library, Baltimore, MD
Catonsville Community College, Catonsville, MD
Dundalk Community College, Dundalk, MD
Simmons College, Boston, MA
Regis College, Newton, MA
Carleton College, Northfield, MN
Meramec Community College, Kirkwood, MO
Missouri Western State College, St. Joseph, MO
Wayne Community College, Goldsboro, NC
New England College, Henniker, NH
Union College, Cransford, NJ

Hamilton College, Clinton, NY
Central Piedmont College, Charlotte, NC
Davidson County Community College, Lexington, NC
Oberlin College, Oberlin, OH
Lane Community College, Ashland, OR
Southern Oregon College, Ashland, OR
Eastern Oregon State College, LaGrande, OR
Franklin & Marshall State College, Lancaster, PA
E. Stroudsburg State College, Stroudsburg, PA
Winthrop College, Rock Hill, SC
Shelby State Community College, Memphis, TN
Del Mar College, Corpus Christi, TX
Weber State College, Ogden, UT
Northern Virginia Community College, Annandale, VA
Paul D. Camp Community College, Franklin, VA
Redford College, Redford, VA
Richard Bland College, Petersburg, VA
St. Michaels College, Winoski, VT
University of Arizona, Tucson, AZ
University of California, Berkeley, CA
University of California, Los Angeles, CA
University of Guelph, Guelph, Ontario, Canada
Denver University, Denver, CO
Colorado State University, Fort Collins, CO
University of Northern Colorado, Greeley, CO
Fairfield University, Fairfield, CT
University of Florida, Gainesville, FL
University of South Florida, Tampa, FL
Georgia Institute of Technology, Atlanta, GA
Boise State University, Boise, ID
University of Idaho, Moscow, ID
Southern Illinois University, Carbondale, IL
University of Illinois, Chicago and Peoria, IL
Loyola University, Chicago, IL
Northwestern University, Evanston, IL
Indiana University, Bloomington, IN
Kansas State University, Manhattan, KS
Wichita State University, Wichita, KS
University of Maine at Orono, Orono, ME
University of Maryland, College Park, MD
Clark University, Worcester, MA
University of Michigan, Ann Arbor, MI
University of Detroit, Detroit, MI
University of Minnesota, Minneapolis, MN
University of Nebraska, Omaha, NE
Appalachian State University, Boone, NC
University of Nevada, Reno, Las Vegas, NV
Rutgers University, New Brunswick, NJ
Colgate University, Hamilton, NY
Hofstra University, Hempstead, NY
Cornell University, Ithaca, NY
St. John's University, Jamaica, NY

State University of New York at Stony Brook, NY
North Carolina State University, Raleigh, NC
University of Akron, Akron, OH
University of Cincinnati, Cincinnati, OH
Ohio State University, Columbus, OH
University of Oklahoma, Norman, OK
University of Pittsburgh, Pittsburgh, PA
University of Tennessee at Chattanooga, Chattanooga, TN
University of Tennessee, Martin, TN
University of Tennessee, Nashville, TN
University of Texas, Arlington, TX
Southern Methodist University, Dallas, TX
Utah State University, Logan, UT
University of Utah, Salt Lake City, UT
Virginia Commonwealth University, Richmond, VA
University of Washington, Odegaard Undergraduate Library, Seattle, WA
University of Wisconsin Kenosha, Madison, Eau Claire, WI
Marquette University, Milwaukee, WI

High School Libraries

S.R. Butler High School, Huntsville, AL
Coronado High School, Scottsdale, AZ
Saguaro High School, Scottsdale, AZ
Santa Rita High School, Tucson, AZ
Arcadia High School, Arcadia, CA
Bell Gardens High School, Bell Gardens, CA
Culver City Junior and Senior High School, Culver City, CA
University High School, Irvine, CA
Wilson High School, Long Beach, CA
Tamalpais High School, Mill Valley, CA
Rowland High School, Rowland Heights, CA
San Gorgonio High School, San Bernadino, CA
Patrick Henry High School, San Diego, CA
San Gabriel High School, San Gabriel, CA
Santa Barbara High School, Santa Barbara, CA
San Rafael High School, San Rafael, CA
Monroe High School, Sepulveda, CA
Palmer High School, Colorado Springs, CO
Darien High School, Darien, CT
Greenwich High School, Greenwich, CT
Ridgefield High School, Ridgefield, CT
Brandon High School, Brandon, FL
Coral Senior High School, Miami, FL
Charlotte High School, Punta Gordo, FL
Sioux City High Schools, Sioux City, IA
Deerfield High School, Deerfield, IL
Hinsdale Township High School, South & Central, Darien & Hinsdale, IL
Lake Forest High School East, Lake Forest, IL
New Trier High School West, Northfield, IL
Brookline High School, Brookline, MA
West Bloomfield High School, Orchard Lake, MI

Minnetonka High School, Excelsior, MN
Anoka High School, Anoka, NM
Horace Greeley High School, Chappaqua, NY
Sayville High School, Sayville, NY
Smithtown High School West, Smithtown, NY
White Plains High School, White Plains, NY
Benson Polytechnic High School, Portland, OR
Haverford High School, Haverford, PA
West Linn High School, West Linn, OR
Bethel Park High School, Bethel Park, PA
Mt. Anthony High School, Bennington, VT
Charlottesville High School, Charlottesville, VA
Petersburg High School, Petersburg, VA
J.R. Tucker High School, Richmond, VA

Special Libraries

Walter Reed Army Hospital, Washington, DC
University of Florida Medical Library, Gainesville, FL
Medical College of Georgia, Augusta, GA
Shawnee Mission School District, Shawnee Mission, KS
University of Kentucky Medical Library, Lexington, KY
Louisiana State University, Medical Libraries, New Orleans and Baton Rouge, LA
National Institute of Health, Bethesda, MD
Wayne State University Law Library, Detroit, MI
Wayne State University Medical Library, Detroit, MI
University of Minnesota, Biomedical Library, Minneapolis, MN
Creighton University Health & Science Library, Omaha, NE
University of Albuquerque, Albuquerque, NM
State University of New York at Buffalo, Law School Library, Buffalo, NY
Nassau Medical Center, East Meadow, NY
University of North Carolina, Health Science Lab, Chapel Hill, NC
Duke University Medical Library, Durham, NC
University of Cincinnati, Health Sciences Library, Cincinnati, OH
University of Oregon Architecture & Allied Arts Library, Eugene, OR
University of Oregon Health Science & Law Libraries, Portland and Eugene, OR
University of Oregon Law Library, Eugene, OR
University of Oregon Medical School, Health Sciences Library, Portland, OR
Oregon Institute of Technology, Klamath, OR
University of Tennessee Law Library, Knoxville, TN
Houston Academy of Medicine, Houston, TX
University of Utah, Health & Science Library, Salt Lake City, UT
Dana Medical Library, University of Vermont, Burlington, VT
University of Virginia Fine Arts Library, Charlottesville, VA
Union Theological Seminary, Richmond, VA
Virginia Commonwealth University, Medical Library, Richmond, VA
Washington State University, Pullman, WA
    Education Library
    Humanities Library
    Science Library
    Social Science Library

Selected Bibliography

Allred, John. "Reticent About Theft." *Library Association Record* 81:85 (February 1979).

"A New Kind of Inventory." *Library Journal* 42:369-71 (May 1917).

"Amnesty Week Reaps 12,000 Overdue Books." *Feliciter* 21:8 (June 1975).

Anson, Brooke. "Foil That Audiovisual Thief!" *Wisconsin Library Bulletin* 74:168+ (July 1978).

Antiquarian Booksellers' Association. *Book Theft From Libraries.* London: Antiquarian Booksellers' Association, 1972.

Archival Security: New Approaches to An Old Problem. Chicago: Society of American Archivists, n.d.

Archival Security Newsletter (March 1977).

"Archival Security Surveys." *Archival Security Newsletter* 6 (July 1976).

Armstrong, Norma, E.S. "Essentials of Library Security—The Librarian's View." *SLA News* 144:51-57 (1978).

"Art Works Stolen From Two New England Libraries." *Library Journal* 100:1592 (September 15, 1975).

Banerjee, D.N. "Inventory Control." *Herald of Library Science* 15:36-41 (January 1976).

Beach, Allyne and Kaye Gapen. "Library Book Theft: A Case Study." *College and Research Libraries* 38:118-28 (March 1977).

Beck, R.E. and J.R. McKinnon. "Development of Methods and Time Standards for a Large Scale Library Inventory." In *Case Studies in Systems Analysis in a University Library.* Barton R. Burkhalter, ed. Metuchen, NJ: Scarecrow Press, 1968, pp. 48-75.

Beckman, Margaret. *Report on Effectiveness of Book Detection System,* McLaughlin Library, University of Guelph, Canada, September 28, 1973.

"Bedeviled Libraries—Is It Bibliomania?" *Mississippi Library News* 42:75+ (June 1978).

Berkeley, Edmund, Jr. "Code of Virginia Revised to Benefit Librarians and Archivists." *Virginia Librarian* 21:18, 19 (May 1975).

Bluh, Pamela. "A Study of an Inventory." *Library Resources and Technical Services* 13:367-71 (Summer 1969).

Bolte, Bill. "Kentucky Librarians' Attitudes on Inventory." *Kentucky Library Association Bulletin* 39:14-18 (Spring 1975).

Bommer, Michael and Bernard Ford. "A Cost-Benefit Analysis for Determining the Value of an Electronic Security System." *College and Research Libraries* 35:270-79 (July 1974).

"Book Theft Control Follows Museum Loss." *Library Journal* 97:3108 (October 1, 1972).

"Book Theft on the Upswing." *Library Journal* 100:2203 (December 1, 1975).

Boss, Richard W. "The Library Security Myth." *Library Journal* 105:683 (March 15, 1980).

Braden, Irene A. "Pilot Inventory of Library Holdings." *ALA Bulletin* 62:1129-31 (October 1968).

Broadhead, R.M. "Comment." *New Library World* 74:236 (1973).

"Brooklyn Security Men Crack Down on Mutilation." *Library Journal* 87:3983 (November 1, 1962).

Burdenuk, Eugene. "Secondary School Cuts Library Pilfering." *Canadian Library Journal* 31:386-91 (September/October 1974).

Burns Women Guards. Briarcliff Manor, NY: Burns International Security Services, n.d.

"Burgers for Overdues." *Library Journal* 105:669 (March 15, 1980).

"Busting the Mexico City Connection." *American Libraries* 10:224 (May 1979).

Clark, J.B. "An Approach to Collection Inventory." *College and Research Libraries* 35:350-53 (September 1974).

Clark, Robert F. and G. Haydee. "Your Charging System: Is It Thiefproof?" *Library Journal* 91:642, 643 (February 1, 1966).

"Cleveland Book Heist: Building Design Blamed." *Library Journal* 100:1173 (June 15, 1975).

"College Stores Lose Heavily to Thieves." *Chronicle of Higher Education,* May 5, 1980, p. 1+.

Crawshaw, Ralph S. "The Tattletape Tale." *JAMA* 239:621-22 (February 13, 1978).

Cummings, J.L. "A Year of Electronic Security." *The Australian Library Journal* 22:142-48 (May 1973).

Cunliffe, Vera. "Inventory of Monographs in a University Library." *Library Resources and Technical Services* 21:72-76 (Winter 1977).

"Don't Mess With This Library." *The Morning Call,* February 4, 1979, pp. A-8.

"Door Locks and Archival Security." *Archival Security Newsletter* (January 1977), n.p.

"Electronic Detection System Reduces Losses in Library." *American School and University* 46:10 (September 1976).

"Experiment in Unsupervised Use of Legal Treatises Fails at University of Texas, Tarlton Law Library." *Law Library Journal* 61:161 (1968).

Fagerhaugh, Kenneth H. "Library Security: Carnegie-Mellon Experience." *Wilson Library Bulletin* 46:856-57 (1972).

"$500 Fines at CPL." *Library Journal* 104:1510 (August 1979).

"A Fortune in Books at the Dump." *The Sun,* April 6, 1979, p. 1.

"Frequency of Inventory." *Library Journal* 52:827, 828 (September 1, 1927).

Fuller, Florine and Irene Glaus. "To Have or Not to Have a Security System." *Tennessee Librarian* 26:41, 44 (Spring 1974).

Garfield, Eugene. "Highly Cited Articles: Human Psychology and Behavior." *Current Contents* (Social and Behavioral Science) 7, no. 18, pp. 5-11.

Garoogian, Andrew. "Making Book at the Reference Desk." *Library Journal* 103:1234-35 (June 15, 1978).

Gertman, Susan. "Security Hardware." *American Bookseller* (November 1979).

Giusto, Joann. "3M's Tattle-Tape Squeals on Bookstore Shoplifters." *Publishers Weekly* 215:34-6 (January 1, 1979).

"Grand Larceny." *Wilson Library Bulletin* 53:617 (May 1979).

Grannis, Chandler B. "1979 Title Output and Average Prices: Preliminary Figures." *Publishers Weekly* 217:54-8 (February 22, 1980).

Greany, William J. *An Investigation Into the Problem of Lost and Damaged Books in the Senior High School Libraries of Suffolk County.* Brookville, NY: Long Island University, 1967.

Greenaway, Emerson. *Checkpoint Security System for Book Theft Prevention: Interim Report.* Philadelphia: Free Library of Philadelphia, 1968.

Griffith, J.W. "Library Thefts: A Problem That Won't Go Away." *American Libraries* 9:224-27 (April 1978).

"He Never Read a Book That He Could Return." *Allentown Morning Call,* August 30, 1977, sect. 1, p. 1.

Hines, Theodore C. "Theft Mutilation and the Loss-to-Use Ratio." *Library Security Newsletter* 1:1-4 (May/June 1975).

Hoel, Paul G. and Raymond J. Jessen. *Basic Statistics for Business and Economics.* New York: John Wiley & Sons, 1971.

Holt, Raymond L. "Commentary." *Library Security Newsletter* 1:7-8 (September/October 1975).

Huttner, Marian A. "Measuring and Reducing Book Losses." *Library Journal* 98:512, 513 (February 15, 1973).

Hyman, Richard Joseph. *Access to Library Collections.* Metuchen, NJ: Scarecrow Press, 1972.

Insko, Don D. "Sophisticated Security System Installed at University of Wyoming Science and Coe Libraries." *Wyoming Library Roundup* 31:23 (March 1976).

"Instructor Admits Book Thefts." *AB* 63:3484 (May 7, 1979).

"Inventories of Books." In *Encyclopedia of Library and Information Science.* v. 13. New York: Marcel Dekker, 1975, pp. 1-3.

"Inventory, Insurance and Accounting." In *A Survey of Libraries in the United States.* v. 4. Chicago: American Library Association, 1927, pp. 119-132.

"Inventory: Report of the ALA Committee on Library Administration." *ALA Bulletin* 3:207, 208 (1909).

"Iowa Throws the Book at Thieves." *Library Journal* 104:1510 (August 1979).

Jaeckel, Christopher C. "Manuscripts: Growing Problem of Thefts." *AB* 63:3858-60 (May 21, 1979).

Jerome, Frank A. "Inventory Maintenance Management of AV Aid Equipment." *Audiovisual Instruction* 20:98-99 (March 1975).

Kaske, Neal K. *A Study of Book Detection Systems' Effectiveness and the Levels of Missing Material at the University of California at Berkeley.* Berkeley: University of California Press, 1978.

Katzenstein, Herbert. "Guidelines for Security of AV Equipment." *Library Security Newsletter* 1:9 (July 1975).

Kinney, John M. "Archival Security and Insecurity." *The American Archivist* 38:493-97 (October 1975).

Kneebone, Ted. "Library Materials That Go AWOL, or the Issue of Security in Illinois Academic Libraries." *Illinois Libraries* 57:338-43 (May 1975).

Knight, Nancy H. "Library Security Systems Come of Age." *American Libraries* 9:229-32 (April 1978).

Knight, Nancy H., ed. "Theft Detection Systems for Libraries: A Survey." *Library Technology Reports* 12:575-690 (November 1976).

Knight, Nancy H. "Theft Detection Systems Revisited: An Updated Survey." *Library Technology Reports* 15:221-409 (May/June 1979).

Langmead, Stephen and Margaret Beckman. *New Library Design: Guide Lines to Planning Academic Library Buildings.* New York: John Wiley & Sons, 1976.

"LAPL Lowers the Boom on Book Thefts." *Library Journal* 95:20 (January 1, 1970).

Lehigh University Forum. Library Subcommittee of the Budget and Priorities, Planning and Resources Committees. "Synopsis of Professor Lindgren's statement in favor of his and Mr. Flato's motion of 7 December 1972." Bethlehem, PA: Lehigh University, 1972.

"Libraries Hit by Book and Art Thefts." *Library Journal* 102:1446, 1447 (July 1977).

Library Security Newsletter 1:10 (March 1975).

"Library Security Roundup." *Library Journal* 98: 1533, 1534 (May 15, 1973).

"Loss of Rare Books Probed at Harvard." *Chronicle of Higher Education* (March 24, 1980).

"Losses Demand Electronics." *Library Association Record* 80:323 (July 1978).

McCarthy, Patricia. "They Shelved Media Openly." *Wisconsin Library Bulletin* 72:29-30 (January-February 1976).

"Mail Box." *AB* 48:1756, 1757 (December 6, 1971).

Mangino, Arlene. "Inventory: Luxury or Necessity?" *Wilson Library Bulletin* 52:574 (March 1978).

"Marking Manuscripts At the Library of Congress." *Archival Security Newsletter* (March 1976) p.6.

Mason, Philip P. "Archival Security: New Solutions to an Old Problem." *The American Archivist* 38:477-92 (October 1975).

"Mexican ILL Book Theft: Libraries Can Recoup Losses." *Library Journal* 104:1207 (June 1, 1979).

Miller, Bruce and Marilyn Sorum. "A Two Stage Sampling Procedure for Estimating the Proportion of Lost Books in a Library." *The Journal of Academic Librarianship* 3:74-80 (1977).

"Minnesota's Carleton College Reports Rare Book Theft." *Library Journal* 104:1097 (May 15, 1979).

Monnelly, Margaret. "Library Security in a High School: Is It Feasible?" *Moccasin Telegraph* 20:5 (Winter 1978).

Moore, Robert S. "Missing Monographs in the Olin Library: A Preliminary Report." *Cornell University Library Bulletin* 210:1-5 (October 1978).

Morley, William F.E. "Security . . . or Defacement?" *Canadian Library Journal* 35(6): 421-25 (December 1978).

Mott, Sharon. "An Edmonton High School Reduces Book Losses." *Canadian Library Journal* 35:45 (February 1978).

Murfin, Marjorie E. and Clyde Hendrick. "Ripoffs Tell Their Story." *The Journal of Academic Librarianship* 1:8-12 (May 1975).

"Music Scores Stolen From Pittsburgh's Carnegie." *Library Journal* 102:1447 (July 1977).

"Mutilation in the Young Adult Section." *Library Security Newsletter* 2:5 (Spring 1976).

Myller, Rolf. *The Design of the Small Public Library*. New York: R.R. Bowker Co., 1966.

"Nail Down Your OCLC Terminal." *Library Journal* 104:1207 (June 1, 1979).

National Survey on Library Security. New York: Burns Security Institute, 1973.

"New Mexico University Library: Site of Book Heist." *Library Journal* 98:1866 (June 15, 1973).

"New Products." *Library Security Newsletter* 1:14 (January 1975).

"New Products." *Library Security Newsletter* 1:15 (January 1975).

"New Products." *Library Security Newsletter* 1:19 (September-October 1975).

"New Search Room Regulations at the North Carolina Division of Archives and History." *Archival Security Newsletter* 6 (November 1975).

"News Notes." *AB* 48:370 (August 16-30, 1971).

Nightingale, John. "Book Losses." *Library Association Record* 77:222-23 (September 1975).

Niland, Powell and William H. Kurth. "Estimating Lost Volumes in a University Library Collection." *College and Research Libraries* 37:132 (March 1976).

"No Fines and Tall Tales." *Library Journal* 104:1207 (June 1, 1979).

Norman, Ronald V. "A Method of Estimating Losses of Checked Out Material." *Nebraska Library Association Quarterly* 9:31-34 (Fall 1978).

Nwamefor, Ralph. "Security Problems of University Libraries in Nigeria." *Library Association Record* 26:244, 245 (December 1974).

O'Neil, James W. "Strengthen Your Security Posture." *Library Security Newsletter* 1:7-9 (March 1975).

Pavlodarskii, A. "A Law for All." *Bibliotekar* (Moscow) 3:48-50 (1979).

"Periodical Mutilation Zooms." *Library Journal* 100:1172 (June 15, 1975).

"Periodical Theft/Mutilation Reported to be Relieved by Microform Conversion." *Library Security Newsletter* 2:20 (Spring 1976).

"Perspiring Periodicals Thief." *American Libraries* 3:228 (March 1972).

Powell, John W. "Architects, Security Consultants and Security Planning for New Libraries." *Library Security Newsletter* 1:1, 6-8 (September/October 1975).

"Preventive Medicine." *Library Journal* 102:1447 (July 1977).

"Princeton Cuts Acquisitions; Theft on the Upswing." *Library Journal* 103:917 (May 1, 1978).

"Protecting Art Exhibits." *Library Security Newsletter* 2(2):11 (Summer 1978).

"Quick! Tell Me How to Buy Library Security Systems." *American School Board Journal* 164:43 (August 1977).

"Rare Book Stealing in Russia." *Library Journal* 103:2153 (November 1, 1978).

"RBMS Manuscript Collections Committee." *Library of Congress Information Bulletin* 35:574-76 (September 17, 1976).

Rendell, Kenneth W. "The Marking of Books and Manuscripts." *AB* 61:676-78 (January 30, 1978).

"Retailers Begin to Feel Economic Pinch as Inflation Erodes Sales Gains." *Publishers Weekly* 216:58-62 (August 20, 1979).

Revill, Don. "Library Security." *New Library World* 79:75-77 (April 1978).

Richmond, Michael L. "Attitudes of Law Librarians to Theft and Mutilation Control Methods." *Law Library Journal* 68:60-70 (February 1, 1975).

"Roanoke and Southwest Virginia: Security Systems and Other Activities." *Virginia Librarian* 21:12 (October 1975).

Roberts, Matt. "Guards, Turnstiles, Electronic Devices and the Illusion of Security." *College and Research Libraries* 29:259-75 (July 1968).

"Rochester Pegs Book Losses." *Library Journal* 105:668 (March 15, 1980).

Romeo, Louis J. "Electronic Theft Detection Systems. Part I: The Small College Libraries." *Library and Archival Security* 2:1 + (1978).

Rovelstad, Mathilde V. "Open Shelves/Closed Shelves in Research Libraries." 37:457-67 (September 1976).

"Safe Mss. Marking Ink Developed by LC." *Library Journal* 102:1806 (September 15, 1977).

Samuel, Evelyn. "Protection of Library and Archival Materials." *Library and Archival Security* 2(3/4):1-6 (1978).

Sanner, Marian. "Pratt Takes Inventory." *Journal of Cataloging and Classification* 11:125-32 (July 1955).

Schindler, Pat. "The Use of Security Guards in Libraries." *Library Security Newsletter* 2:1-6 (Summer 1978).

"Security Badges in Milwaukee." *Library Journal* 102:1230 (June 1, 1977).

"Security in Libraries." *Library Journal* 103:2292 (November 15, 1978).

"Security in Libraries." *Library Journal* 104:878 (April 15, 1979).

"Security in Libraries." *Library Journal* 104:1206 (June 1, 1979).

"Security Person at Bettendorf." *Library Journal* 105:345 (February 1, 1980).

"Selling Goods is Better than Losing Them." *Nation's Business* 67:64, 65 (October 1979).

"Seven Rutgers University Libraries Protect Books . . ." News Release, St. Paul, MN: 3M, n.d.

Shearer, Sergeant Alex. "Essentials of Library Security—The Police View." *SLA News* 144:43-47 (1978).

Sheridan, Robert N. "Keeping the Books." *Wilson Library Bulletin* 51:296-99 (December 1976).

Sheridan, Robert N. "Measuring Book Disappearance." *Library Journal* 99:2040-43 (September 1, 1974).

Sheridan, Robert N. and P.W. Martin. *Results of Tests Conducted to Determine the Need for a Book Theft Deterrent Device.* Levittown, NY: Levittown Public Library, 1972.

Sherman, Jake. "Book Theft: How Bad a Problem for Vermont Libraries?" *Vermont Libraries* 3:16-19 (September/October 1974).

Sivertz, Chloe T. "Inventory Up to Date." *Wilson Library Bulletin* 26:68, 69 (September 1951).

"60-College Security Study Finds Few Satisfied." *Library Journal* 93:1848 (May 1, 1968).

Smith, Hardin E. "Taking Inventory." *Library Journal* 87:2847, 2848 (September 1, 1962).

"Sorry, Wrong Number." *Library Security Newsletter* 2:11 (March 1975).

Souter, G.H. "Delinquent Readers: A Study of the Problem in University Libraries." *Journal of Librarianship* 8:101 (April 1976).

"Stanford's Book Heist." *Library Journal* 101:2418 (December 1, 1976).

"Surveillance Systems for School Media Centers." *Wilson Library Bulletin* 48:529-30 (March 1974).

Survey of Libraries in the United States. v. 4. Chicago: American Library Association, 1927, pp. 130-31.

"10,000 Stolen Books Found." *Library Association Record* 80:266 (June 1978).

"Theft in San Francisco." *Library Journal* 104:1207 (June 1, 1979).

"Theft Prevention." *Library Journal* 102:1328 (June 15, 1977).

"Theft Via Stolen Identification." *Library Journal* 101:768 (March 15, 1976).

Thompson, Earle C. "LJ's Survey of Accession and Inventory Practices." *Library Journal* 84:1048-52 (April 1, 1959).

Thompson, Lawrence S. "New Reflections on Bibliokleptomania." *Library Security Newsletter* 1:8, 9 (January 1975).

Thompson, Lawrence S. "Notes on Bibliokleptomania." *The New York Public Library Bulletin* 48:723-60 (September 1944).

"Tough Security Measures Adopted by Research Libraries." *Library Journal* 101:764 (March 15, 1976).

"Tracing Stolen Books: *BW* Offers Ad Space." *Library Journal* 102:1806 (September 15, 1977).

"Truancy Procedures at Baltimore County Public Library." *Library Security Newsletter* 1:11 (January 1975).

Tyler, Carol W. "Book Theft: A Brief Review." *Cornell University Library Bulletin* 1:9-12 (October-December 1976).

"UB Library Losses to be Detailed Soon." *Buffalo Evening News*, October 3, 1979, p. 39.

"Unconditional Amnesty." *Library Journal* 100:1172 (June 15, 1975).

Ungarelli, Donald L. "Excerpts—Taken From a Paper Entitled *The Empty Shelves." Bookmark* 32:155 (May/June 1973).

United States Code. Title 20. Sect. 351. Washington: Government Printing Office, 1970.

"University of Toronto Settles Access Issue." *Library Journal* 97:2140 (June 15, 1972).

"Video Monitor OK'D by Illinois Library." *Library Journal* 95:113 (January 15, 1970).

Vincent, Ida. "Electronic Security Systems in Libraries: Measuring the Costs and Benefits." *The Australian Library Journal* 27:231 (September 1978).

Von Schon, C.V. "Inventory by Computer." *College and Research Libraries* 38:147-52 (March 1977).

Walch, Timothy. *Archives and Manuscripts: Security.* (Basic Manual Series). Chicago: Society of American Archivists, 1977.

Walch, Timothy. "The Improvement of Library Security." *College and Research Libraries* 38:100-103 (March 1977).

Walsh, Robert R. "Rare Book Theft and Security System Confidentiality." *Library and Archival Security* 2(3/4):24-25 (1978).

Watkins, Beverly T. "College Stores Lose Heavily to Thieves." *Chronicle of Higher Education* 20:1+ (May 5, 1980).

Welch, Thomas J. "An Approach to an Inventory of the Collections." *Library Resources and Technical Services* 21:77-80 (Winter 1977).

"We Paint Stripes on Our Periodicals." *Southeastern Librarian* 20:195 (Fall 1970).

Weyhrauch, Ernest E. and Mary Thurman. "Turnstiles, Checkers and Library Security." *Southeastern Librarian* 18:111-15 (Summer 1968).

Wheeler, Joseph L. and Herbert Goldhor. *Practical Administration of Public Libraries.* New York: Harper & Row, 1962.

"The Worse They Get." *Wilson Library Bulletin* 50:217 (November, 1976).

"Yale and Newberry Recover Stolen Maps." *American Libraries* 10:100 (March 1979).

Index

About the Author

Alice Harrison Bahr is the author of numerous monographs in Knowledge Industry Publications' Professional Librarian series, including *Book Theft and Library Security Systems, 1978-79, Automated Library Circulation Systems, 1979-80* and *Video in Libraries, 1979-80.* A graduate of Temple University, she holds an M.L.S. from Drexel University and an M.A. and Ph.D. from Lehigh University. Ms. Bahr is project librarian/government publications at Muhlenberg College Library.